TALENT EMPLOYEE TRAINING METHOD

JOHN LOK

ISBN 979-888629083-7

Contents

Preface

Preface

I write this book aims to let interviewers to know why to apply pshological methods to judge how to choose the most suitable applicant(s) more accurate to any organization in any interviews. This book consists three chapters.

The first chapter indicates what the common interviews are as well as explains why interviewers need to apply psychological methods to test any applicant behaviors in any interview process.

The second chapter explains how to apply psychological recruitment strategies effect/manage in the recruitment process to achieve more effective and efficient interview as well as explains how to apply occupational psychological test method to test applicant's ability.

The third chapter how selection assessment methods are applied to choose the best applicants to achieve the most effective and efficient interview result as well as how to criteria for selecting and evaluating assessment methods in interview which are the most reasonable support.

I write this book final chapter explains whether training program must be either needed to any organizations in order to raise productivities, efficiencies or improve performance etc. different aspects effect to be beneficial to any organization or waste money and time to spend training program expenditures.

Do any kinds of organizations must be beneficial, such as raise employees' efficiencies, productivities and improve performance after any training programs are arranged to be trained to trainees from their training department's trainers? Is any kind of training program useful to any organization ? How to find and design the best suitable training program to satisfy every employee individual need in any organization?

In this final chapter, I shall give my opinions to attempt to answer these above questions. In final chapter,. I shall give one organization training case study to explain how my reasons are supported my conclusion. Finally, I expect my readers can learn how to design any training courses to attribute beneficial needs to your employees and organizations.

The chapter five explains these questions : How can talent human be created successful? What are the differences between talent human and common human IQ? How to evaluate the person has special talented human and excellent abilities? What aspects do we need to train talent human to attribute our society? Which kinds of talent human shortage to our society nowadays?

Our future will need different kinds of talent human to attribute their abilities to let our society to develop in success. So, future talent skillful training is very important . If our future society can train talent human in success, then our society will have more chance to achieve any unpossible missions, e.g. Mar living exploration, undiscovered natural resource exploration, artificial intelligent technological development, new medical medicine invention etc. different missions, which is waiting our talent humans attribute their unique knowledge to achieve these any one of missions in success. Hence, talent human training is essential. How can we train talent human in success. We must know what methods will have possible to achieve training any kinds of talent human in success.

In chapter six, I shall suggest methods how to measure what the level of employee satisfaction . Supermarket organization will be indicated to be one case to explain how to measure what the level of employee satisfaction. I shall also indicate how leaders can satisfy employee needs. I shall explain the satisfactory methods to give recommendation from the organization's and staff's point of both view. I shall indicate how makes one company more successful than another. I shall apply agency theory and Mallow's Basic needs to give evidences to let readers can have more confidence to understand how to satisfy employee's individal needs.I shall indicate what system approach is and how different organizational workplace environments will influence staff's different variable causes to decide how to do whole daily behaviors, how to fit to work in the organization when the organization can apply system approach to satisfy employee's needs more easily. I shall explain how organization can satisfy to employees easily from different psychological factors. I shall explain how to achieve work motivation strategy to raise employee productivities. I shall explain what can influence organizational behaviors to satisfy employee's individual needs to achieve to raise performance efficiently.

This book aims to let readers to learn how to apply psychological methods to let employees feel satisfactory to enjoy to do their job in order to raise productivity and improve performance. This book will indicate some methods to explain how to achieve training talent human plan in success. It is suitable to any readers have interest to know what methods can train talent human in possible success.

Prologue

Table Of Contents

and how to solve

● Prediction rewards and costs of training program
● Can train employees raise efficiency
Chapter Three
Training Super Talent
Human Methods

● The talent management skill raises organizational development and motivation of employees

● Talent in the world of work meaning
● Building high performance culture talent management method to organizations
● Non-training method creates talent young people
Chapter Four
Employee Psychological Research
Employee satisfaction measurement
● How to measure employee satisfaction ?

● How can leaders satisfy employee needs?

Raising employee efficiency
● How does one company raise employee efficiency

Organizational behavior theory
● What is system approach?

Employee satisfaction methods
● How can satisfy to employees' needs?
● How to achieve work motivation strategy ?

- How can influence organizational positive behaviors ?
  Reference

CHAPTER ONE

Interview psychology methods

What are common psychology methods of recruitment choice?

Can any psychology methods are used to choose who will be the best recruitment applicant(s) in any recruitment stage more accurate? Can the interviewer observe the applicant's psychological phenomenon to judge whether the applicant can be the best or the most suitable applicant in the recruitment stage more accurate? To answer above these questions. We need to know why a systematic scientific procedure is an essential component to achieve any psychological method(s) to test candidate individual ability to judge whether who is the best or the most suitable applicant to do any position in any organization.

A psychologist can follow a systematic scientific procedure which has theoretical base in order to explain and interpret the psychological phenomenon of the applicant to decide whether who is the best or the most suitable applicant to do the position in the organization.

On the one hand, in order to obtain the applicant's psychological response from individual applicant, there are a number of psychological tools or instruments are used during the interview process. The responses are taken on these tools constitute the basic data which are analyzed to study the applicant experiences, e.g. working experiences, life experiences, mental processes and behaviors. On the other hand, in order to understand every applicant's behavior during the interview process. The different psychological methods can be applied for solving different applicant's individual behavior (individual mental problems) to judge who will be the best or the most suitable applicant to the position in any organization. Because different situations will cause the applicant to choose how to do or perform different behaviors to persuade the interviewer believes who is the best or the most suitable applicant to do the position in the organization. Thus, whose performances will be shaped by many factors both intrinsic and extrinsic to him or her in any interview process.

The common psychological methods of interview process include such as: For observation psychological method example, when shopping in the market , the researcher must have noticed various activities of the consumers . When he/she observes the consumers their activities, the researcher also think about as to why who are doing those activities and probably the researcher reaches a conclusion about the causes of such activities. So, observation is as a psychological method of enquiry is often understand as a systematic registering of events without any deliberate attempt to interface with variables operating in the event which is being studies.

Thus, observation psychological method seems to be applied to judge who is the best or the most suitable applicant to do any position in any organization in any interview process. Such as in any interview process, the interviewer (observer) can use this method to judge or observe every applicant's face and behavioral performance to feel whether who is the best or the most suitable applicant who own ability or confidence or qualification or experience to already to do the job to achieve the recruitment result is more accurate. For example, the interviewer (observer) can attempt to give one simple or difficult task to test whether whom the applicant has the more effort of the induced stress on task performance in the short time observation test in the on part stage of the interview process.

However, observation is also divided into either participant or non-participant both types, depending on the role of observer (interviewer). In the case of interview participant observation, the interviewer mixes up with the job (task) performance event test under study and conducts concerns the interview test, e.g. group discussion interview test, the applicants and the interviewer will discuss one or more than one topic(s) which concern(s) on relating the position requirement issue. So, the interviewer can analyze whom applicant(s) can talk the most reasonable evidences to support whose opinions to argue the topic against the other applicants together among of them in the short time group discussion, e.g. between 15 minutes to 30 minutes. It aims to let the interviewer can have enough time to record whose opinions to analyze whose opinions are the most reasonable argument to support whose main points to win this position among these interview competitors in the short time group discussion.

Thus, the interviewer needs to participate the group discussion to ask every applicant any questions and let them to attempt to solve any challenges in the whole group discussion. After the group discussion, then the interviewer can have more effort or confidence to judge whom applicant (s) is/are the most suitable or the best applicant (s) to do the job for his/ her organization more accurate.

Otherwise, as in the case of interview non-participant observation, the interviewer maintains an optimum distance and has little impact on the interview event. Such as the interview group discussion test. The interviewer won't ask any questions to let the applicants to attempt to answer. Otherwise, he/she will let the applicants have chance to ask any questions or answer the questions among of their discussion related to the topic. So the interviewer's role is a listener, who only needs to listen every applicant how who can ask and can answer any questions to decide who can talk the most correct or the right or the most reasonable answers to answer their questions in the short time group discussion. Then, the interviewer can record all applicants' questions and answers to make the judgement to decide who will be the right or the most suitable applicant to do the position in her/him organization more accurate.

Why does need to test the applicant's psychological behavior in the interview process?

To answer this question, we need to know why any large or middle size organizations which need have human resource department. To challenge of today's HR managers is to create a pool of good employees in the organization. It starts from selection process of the employees. So, interview has been used as an important selection method by HR managers for long time. The cost of rehiring the importance of hiring the right person for right position first. It requires a reliable and valid interview process. Although, any interview won't guarantee 100 percent success in hiring the best employees into any organization, but the proper application is at least, will improve the chances of hiring the best applicant for the job the organization. The importance is given to the selection of right employees for the right positions. Firms are now realizing the value of the good employees because who can make a difference through their job performance. So, various selection methods are now being used to identify the right candidate.

“ Interview” has emerged as a very useful tool in this regard. It is a very common selection method and has a high predictive validity for job performance (Robertson, & Smith , 2001). The main purpose of the interview is to select the right candidate for the right job. The importance of conducting an effective interview is also rising. So consensus was found among the HR experts regarding the effective interview techniques. There are a number of existing literatures regarding the techniques of an effective interview, but every few literatures exist regarding a systematic approach of conducting exist regarding a systematic approach of conducting an effective interview.

This is a very few literatures exist regarding a complete interview process that shows a clear path to the employers for selecting right employees. A lot of interview technique are available, but the problem arises regarding the use of these techniques in a concrete manner. A systematic approach of interview will facilitate the tasks of HR managers in selecting the right applicant for the right position.

(Stevens, 1997) author indicated the whole process of the interview has been described in terms of “3D”- Development, discussion and decision. This study is particularly important for three reasons. First , it will help the HR mangers to think about the employee selection interview in a concrete manner. Second, it will help them to use a number of interview techniques in an effective way that will ultimately increase the chance of hiring the right person for the right position. Third, it will enrich the existing literature of selection interview.

(Stevens, 1997) author also explained that the growing importance of good employees will cause a challenge to the HR managers. The selection process of today’s HR manager is becoming complex and challenging. Undoubtedly, the overall aim, of the selection process is to identify the candidates who are suitable for the vacancy or wider requirement of the HR plan. “ Interview” has been used as a ‘ critical selection method ‘ by HR managers. The interview is the most valid method in determining an applicant’s organizational fit, level of motivation and inter-personal selects.

Whetton & Cameron (2002) cited steps of process of conducting an interview, what they named as People-oriented selection interview process. Here is explains the interview process: P=prepare, E=establish rapport, O=obtain information, P=provide information, C= lead top close and E= evaluate.

So, it seems that the candidates' behavior individual performance in the interview process can be predicted whether who is(are) the most suitable or the best to do the position in the organization from the interviewer's observation. So, it also means the candidate's attitude in the interview process can perform to let the interviewer to feel whether who is suitable or the best to do the position in the organization . Thus, observation of the applicant individual performance, it is an interviewer's best interest to find good prospects, hire them and have them stay in the organization.

Therefore, the interviewees are needed to be provided sufficient information about the job and organization to have enough time to prepare before who will go to interview fairly. It aims to let every candidate has enough confidence to prepare to answer any questions in further interview process fairly. So, the development stage is a good preparation for the interview facilitates the effective interview process. To aim to let the candidate have enough preparation to interview , it should begin long before the first question is ever asked fairly.

In conclude, HR department seems an essential department to any middle or large organizations nowadays. It does not attribute only recruitment function to any organization, it also attribute the chance to give one psychological test function to evaluate whom applicant has the more experience and qualification and effort to do any position in any organization. If the interviewer has not prepared any psychological method to test any applicants to judge whether who has the more effort to do the position. Then, I believe the interview result will be more failure and more inaccurate to employ the most suitable applicant , due to who lacks the enough effort and qualification and experience to perform to finish any tasks or duties of the position . So, it is important why any organization needs have good psychological method to test and observe the applicant's psychological behavior in the interview process?

Occupation psychological
test methods
How to apply psychological recruitment
strategies effect/manage in the
recruitment process?

HR (human resource) managers understand accept that poor recruitment decisions continue to affect organizational performance and limit goal achievement. In this case, many jurisdictions to identify and implement new effective hiring strategies will be serious issue to any HR departments to concern.

Acquiring and retaining high-quality talent is critical to any organization's success. So, recruiters need to be more elective in their choice. Since poor recruiting decisions can produce long term negative effects, among their high training and development costs to minimise the incidence of poor performance and high turnover to impact staff morale, the production of high quality goods and services. Thus, HR managers must seek all possible methods for improve their output and provide the satisfaction to their clients require and deserve. The provision of high quality goods and services begins with the recruitment process.

(Schuler, Randalls, 1989) explained recruitment is as " the set of activities and processes used to legally obtain a sufficient number of qualified applicants at the right place and time. So that the applicants and the organization can select each other in their own best short and long term interests.

Thus, it seems that successful recuritment begins with proper employment planning and forecasting. So any one organization needs analyze what kinds of positions of future needs talent available within and outside of the organization and the current and anticipated resources that can be expected to attract and retain such talent. Thus, HR manager needs have one successful strategy to be prepared to employ in order to identify and select the best candidates for its developing pool of human resources.

In common, one successful recuruitment strategy involves these several processes of :

Step one : Development of a policy on recruitment and giving life to the policy.

Step two: Needing assessment to determine the current and future human resource requirement of the organization.

Step three: If the activity is to be effective , the HR requirements for each job category and functional division /unit of the organization must be assessed, identification within and outside the organization of the potential human resources pool.

Step four: Job analysis and job evaluation to identify the individual aspects of each jobs and calculate its relative worth, assessment of qualifications profiles, job descriptions that identify responsibilities and requirement skills, abilities , knowledge and experience, determination to pay salaries and benefits within a defined period.

Step five: identification and documentation of the actual process of recruitment and selection to ensure equity and laws.

Thus, the psychological recruitment strategy for the interviewer includes how to ask interview questions, how to give interview scores and panellists' comments, results of tests (where administered). Because and length of interview time for the interview. There are any interview main contents to any interviewer needs to concern how to arrange interview process.

For example, nowadays, it is popular internet recruiting. Although, interviewer can reduce time to arrange and spend time to interview any applicants, due to the interviewer can interview any applicants from whose organization website . Specially, there are many similar potential interview competitors to apply to the position at the same time. Otherwise, internet recruiting is not all positive. Such as some applicants skill place great value in face-to-face interactons in the hiring process. Such applicant;s are likely to ignre jobs posted, impersonally on time.

I shall indicate these sample recruitment strategy to explain how to influence every applicant's choice to apply the job or not apply the job as below:

The first is online recruiting. This online recuritment strategy has a large percentage of employees are hired by human service agencies for every level jobs are seeking their first career job. The newspaper want ads are not an effective recruitment source for most of today's applicants. Placing vacancy announcements online is more effective and economical than using most traditional forms of advertising. However, online recruitment is designed to close this gap: Not reaching majority of applicants, especially young graduates.

The second is campus recruiting and job fairs. This campus recruiting strategy attracts both professional and paraprofessional applicants, who can be effectively recruited at job fairs sponsored by state workforce development agencies. However, college recruiting can be a very effective method for attracting applicants for professional jobs. The possible psychological advantages to applicants that includes any employers will send team of HR representatives to any colleges to provide an opportunity for job seekers to ask both job specific and hiring process/benefits questions; sending an ambassador to classrooms to quest lecture; schedule experienced employees or supervisors to ask on a hot topic in the human or service field at a local college or university. However, this campus recruiting strategy has a large percentage of employees hired, but need to improve overall applicant.

The third is university partner developing a variety of recruitment strategy. University partnership benefits include to collaborate with university deans and professors to help student interest in the field as well as to develop program partially covering college tuition and other expenses of college students who agree to work for the human service agency for specified periods of time. Its recruitment strategy aims to develop a variety of recruitment strategies with area universities, community colleges and schools of social work to encourage students to pursue careers in the human services. It's weakness lacks enough applicants with specialized social work degrees.

The fourth recruitment strategy is target recruitment. Employers may used a more diverse workforce that better reflects the client population who serve. For example, employers may need to recruit employees with specific lannguage skills or with specialized degrees , e.g. criminal juice. It' weakness lacks of diversity in targeted jobs.

The fifth recruitment strategy is internships. Interns sometimes are paid stipend, but in most instances interns are fulfilling an academic requirement of the college or university. Although supervisors and/or cause work staff must spend time supervising and training interns, the potential payoff is having a known applicant who is familiar with agency operations. Its weakness is needed to improve overall applicant pool.

The sixth recruitment strategy is maintain a pre-screened applicant pool. It has a pool of pre-screened, interviewed applicants always available to be called for a second interview with the hiring supervisor. When, using this approach, it's important to minimize the amount of time between the initial interview and the second interview to prevent top quality applicants from being hired human resources will need to do continuous recruiting and screening , even when there are no current vacancies. It's weaknesses include that some

human services organizations delay hiring until staff vacancies reach crisis proportions. They than initiate a recruitment process that is designed to bring new employees on board as soon as possible . The unfortunate result is hiring employees who meet the minimum requirements, but nothing more. It also has too many applicants get hired with only the minimum credentials.

The seventh recruitment strategy is realistic job previews. Realistic job previews are designed to prevent applicants from taking jobs that who have life knowledge of or are not suited to perform. It is a recruiting tool is designed to reduce early turnover by communicating both the desirable and the undesirable aspects of a jobs before applicants accept a job offer. It can be in the form of videos, oral presentations, job shadowing opportunities. It's weakness includes unwanted turnover among new workers who did not understand their job when who were hired.

The final recruitment strategy is improved hiring flexibilities in highly centralized systems. It means many public-seator human service agencies are regulated by merit systems that make it different to attract and maintain the interest of top-qualify applicants. Top applicants in today's economy are searching the interest for jobs that are available now. They aren't interested in taking a civil service exam and sitting on eligibility lists for months. In some systems requirements and lengthy inflexible scoring processes wash out well qualified applicants. It's weaknesses include hiring process takes too long, high qualify applicants are looking elsewhere for jobs.

How to apply occupational psychological
test method to test applicant's ability?

Occupational psychological interview method is the application of the science of psychology to test applicant individual work ability. For example, any interviews can apply occupational psychologists' test method to attempt to test applicant individual performance, motivation and wellbing of the organization in the workplace. If any interviewers can attempt to apply occupational psychologist test method to test any applicant individual working abilities in interview. It brings this question: How can the interviewer develop, apply and evaluate a range of tools and interventions to test the applicant individual working abilities across many different areas of the workplace?

The occupational psychological test method can include these psychological skills to test every applicant individual ability in interview. Such as : Psychological assessment means selecting and assessing the applicant individual ability using interview enquiring method, e.g. in interview, enquiring applicant concerns on how to solve crisis deal issues when challenges cause in any workplace, assessments of what the applicant's main ability centres are. Situational judgement tests, e.g. how to solve challenges in different situations and personality questionnaires and cognitive ability tests. Profiling jobs are matching requirements to the applicant's future performance. Developing and choosing is valid, reliable, fair and suitable selectin procedures.

Thus, the psychological enquiring questions can concern on work motivation, performance, appraisal and management, leadership power influence and negotiation, employee engagement and commitment, citizenship and positive behaviors or counterproductive in workplace, psychology of group teams and teamwork different aspects, which have similar points , such as concern organizational behavior questions. It aims to test the applicant how to deal any immediate crisis in the organization if the interviewer decides to employ him/her.

The key focus of how to achieve one effective psychological test to the applicant in the interiew. It focuses on key areas , such as the applicant personal goal attainment, interview performance, the applicnt's mind on innovation and creativity aspects, and well being in the workplace how the applicant explains who will perform supposes who did the job in the workplace.

In the interview, the interviewer needs the applicant to explain to let him/her to understand how the applicant's relation and motivation in the organization. The interviewer also needs to know how the applicant can solve any challenges in workplace in the suitation test interview. Because conflict resolution is a challenging environment to work in. However, any downsides are offset by the rewards of being able to help protect both the organization and its employees from the psychological , physiological and economic costs of conflict. Because conflict will occur in possible in any workplaces. Thus, the interviewer ought to ask the question to let him/her to know the applicant will solve if who did this position.

Human factors is a discipline concerned with how the successful interview applicant (future employee) works effectively and safely. It considers a employee's environmental , organizational, job and individual characteristics. These factors will affect the organizational successful interview applicant (future employee) behavior and it is past of the interviewer's job to analyze these and to give recommendations for change to improve human performance to the organization if who selected to employ these applicants in every time interview. Thus it seems occupational psychological test method can give benefits to the interviewer to understand more to the applicants to judge whether who will be the most suitable applicant(s)to do any positions in whose organization more accurate decision in any interviews.

Selecting and evaluating assessment methods

Selection assessment methods

Organizations compete in the war for talent. So, one effective selection assessment method can help any organizations to choose the best applicant(s). Using scientifically proven assessments to make selection decisions, even though such assessments have been shown to result in significant productivity increases, cost savings, decrease other critical organizational outcomes. I shall indicate common misconceptions about selection tests, such as: Screening applicants for conscientiousness will yield better performers , then screening applicants for intelligence, screening applicants for their values will yield better performers , then screening applicants for intelligence, integrity tests are not ueful because job candidates misrepresent themselves on these typs of tests, unstructured interviews with candidates provide better information than structured assessment processes and using selection tests creates legal problems for organizations rather than helps to solve them.

There are numerous different types of formal assessments that organizations can use to select employees. The first step in developing or selecting an assessment method for a given situation is to understand what the job requires employees to do and what knowledge, skills and abilities individuals must posses in order to perform the job effectively. This is typically accomplished by conducting a job analysis . For job oriented job analysis recruitment example, providing test by stating fact and answer questions, gathering and reviewing information to obtain obtain evidence or develop background information on subjects, integrating diverse information to uncover relationships between individuals, events or evidences.

Other assessment methods focus on how measuring the best applicant who are required to perform job tasks effectively, such as various mental abilities, physical abilities or personality traits, depending on the job's requirements. If one were to assess whether candidates could solve decisive and communicate effectively. Alternatively, if one were selecting an administrative assistant, such as the ability to perform work conscientiously with speed and accuracy would be such more important for identifying capable candidates. Some worker-oriented or job analysis data are used as a basis for developing assessment method, that focus on a job candidate's underlying abilities to perform important work task.

In general, any organization interviews only divide either internal or external both selection. Internal selection refers to situations where organization is hiring or promoting from within, whereas, external selection refers to situations where an organization is hiring from the outside. When some assessent methods are used more commonly for external selection. (e.g. cognitive ability tests, personality tests, integrity tests). There are numerous examples of organizations that have used one or more of the following tools for internal selection, external selection or both. I shall explain what the differences for these interview test methods as follow:

What is cognitive ability tests. These assessment measure a variety of mental abilities, such as verbal and mathematical ability, reasoning ability and reading comprehension. Cognitive ability tests have been shown to be extremely useful predictors of job performance and thus are used frequently in making selection decisions for many different types of jobs (Hunter, J. 1986, Ree, M.J. & Teachout, M.S. 1984, Gottredson, L.S. 1982).

Cognitive ability tests typically consist of multipler choice items that are administered via a paper-and-pencil instructment or computer. Some cognitive ability tests contain test items that need various abilities, e.g. verbal ability, numberical ability etc. But then sum up the correct answers to all of the items to obtain a singl total score. The total score then represents a measure of general mental ability. If a separate score is computed for each of the specific types of abilities, then the resulting scores represent measures of the specific mental abilities.

Job knowledge tests mean these assessments measure critical knowledge areas that are needed to perform a job effectively. Typically, the knowledg areas measured represent technical knowledge. Job knowledge tests are used in situations m where candidates must clearly possess a body of knowledge prior to job entry. Job knowledge tests are not appropriate to use in situations where candidates will be trained after selection on the on knowledge areas who need to have. Like cognitive ability tests, job knowledge tests typically consist of multiple-choice items administered via a paper-and-pencil instrument or a computer , although essay items are sometimes included in job knowledg tests (Hunter, J. 1986).

Personality tests that assess traits relevant to job performance have been shown to be effective predictors of subsequent job performance. The personality factors that are assessed most frequently in work situations include conscientiousness, extraversion, agreeableness, openness to experience and emotional stability (Barrick, M.R. & Mount, M.K. 1991, Costa, P.T. Jr., & Mccae, r. R. 1982).

Research has shown that conscientiousness is the most useful predictor of performance across many different jobs. Although some of the other pesonality factors have been shown to be useful predictors of peformance in specific types of jobs (Hough, L.M. 1992). It can consist of several multipe choice or true/false items measuring each personality factor. Like cognitive ability and knowledge tests, which are also administered in a paper-and-pencil or computer format.

Biographical data (biodata) inventories, which ask job candidates questions covering their background, personal characteristics or interests have been shown to be effective predictors of job performance (Stokes, G.S. & Owens, W.A. 1994, Shoenfeldt, L.F. 1999). Another form of a biodata inventory is an instrument called an " accomplishment stored". With this types of assessment, candidates prepare a written account of their most meritorious accomplishments in key skill and ability areas that are required for a job , e.g. planning and organizing, customer service, conflict resolution (Hough, L.M. 1984).

Integrity tests measure attitudes and experiences that are related to an individual honesty, trustworthiness and dependability (Sackett, P.R. & Wanek, J.E. 1996). It is typically multiple-choice in format and administered via a paper-and-pencil instrument or a computer.

Physical fitness tests are used in some selection situations. These tests require candidates to perform general physical activities to assess one's overall fitness, strength or other physical capabilities necessary to perform the job.

Situational judgement tests provide job candidates with situations that who would encounter on the job and viable options for handling the presented situations (Mecichmann, D., Schmitt, N. & Harvey, V.S. 2001). depending on how the test is designed , candidates are asked to select the most effective or most and least effective ways of handling the situaton from the response options provided. Situational judgement tests are more complicated to develop than many of the other types of assessments. It is because more difficulty in developing scenarios with several likely response options that are all viable, but in fact, some are reliably rated as being more effective than others. Situational judgement tests are typically administered in written or paper-and-pencil test booklet or on a computer.

Assessment centers are a type of work sample test that is typically focused on assessing higher-level managerial and supervisory competencies (Thornton, G.C III 1992). Assessment centers usually last at least a day and up to several days. They typically include role-play exercises in -basket exercises, analytical exercises and group discussion exercises. Trained assessors observe the performane of candidates during the assessment process and evaluate them on standardized rating. Some assessment centers also include other types of assessment methods, such as cognitive ability, job knowledge and personality tests. It should be noted selection purposes that assessment centers aren't only used for comprehensive development feedback to participants.

Physical ability tests are used regularly to select workers for physiclly demanding jobs, such as police officers and firefighters. These test are similar to work sample tests in that who typically require candidates to perform a series of actual job tasks to determine whether or not who can perform the physical requirements of a jobs. Physical ability tests are often scored in a pass/fail basis. To pass, the complete set of taks that comprise the test must be properly completed within a specified timeframe.

How to criteria for selecting and evaluating assessment methods in interview?

Properly identifying and implementing formed assessment methods to select employees is one of the more complex areas for HR department to learn about and understand. This is because understanding selection testing requires knowledge of statistics, measurement issues and legal issues relevant to testing.

I recommend any interviewers need to understand important criteria to decide to choose which kind of interview test is the suitable to test applicant individual abilities in every interview such as below:

The first criteria includes validity. Validity means the extent to which the assessment method is useful for predicting subsequent job performance. Adverse impact means the extent to which protected group members , e.g. minorities, females and individualds over 40 score lower on the assessment than majority group members.

The second criteria includes cost. Cost is both to develop and to administer the assessment. Applicant reactions means the extent to which applicants react positively versus negtively to the assessment method. For example, cognitive ability test. on the positive side, this type of assessment is high on validity and low on costs. However, it is also high on adverse impact, moderately favorable. Thus, when cognitive tests are inexpensive and very useful for predicting subsequent job performance, minoritie score significantly lower on them than whites. There is no simple, formulaic approach for selecting " one best" assessment method, because all of them have advantages and disadvantages.

However, the most important consideration in evaluating on assessment method is its validity. Validity refers to whether or not the assessment method provides useful information about how effectively an employee will actually perform once who is hired for a job. Validity is the most important factor in considerating whether or not to use an assessment method because identify who will doesn't accurately identify who will perform effectively on a job has no value to the organization.

There are two major forms of validity: criterion-related validity and content validity is a simple example will illustrate how criterion-related validity can be established. Assume that a sales job requires employees to have a high level of customer service orientation and an organization decides to implement a selection test that assesses prospective applicants on their customer service skills. In order to show that the client skills assessment is a valid predictor of peformance , it must be shown that individuals who score higher on the assessment perform better. On the job and individuals who score lower on the assessment perform less well on the job. Thus, validity in this case would be defined as a meaningful relationship between how well people performed on the assessment and how well who subsequently performed on the job. Content validity approach to validation involves demonstrating that an assessment provides a direct measure of how well candidates will actually perform to job. This type of validation requires analyzing the job to identify the tasks that are performed.

What are the differences between criterion related versus content validation. Criterion-related validity can be used to evaluate the validity of any assessment where individuals receive scores that reflect how well who perform on the test and these scores are subsequently shown to relate to how well who perform on the job. Content validation can only be used to validate assessments that provide a direct measure of how well candidates perform job tasks or the content of the jobs, such as work sample tests. Otherwise, criterion-related validity evidence or contect validity . Thus, it is more desirable to obtain if it is possible to conduct a successful unbiased performance measures must be available. Unfortunately, performance appraisal ratings, which are the most commonly used performance measures can be inaccurate and often fail.

Adverse impact is examined by comparing the proportion of majority group who are selected from a job to the protected group members who are selected. When organizations are and should be interested in selecting the higher quality work force possible, many are also concerned about selecting a diverse workforce ought not using measures that will systematically produce adverse impact against protected groups.

In conclusion, either if an assessment method is shown to produce adverse impact and the organization wished to continue the last of that assessment, there are legal requirements to ensure that the method must have demonstrated validity or if an organization uses an assessment that produces adverse impact that produces adverse impact without the validity evidence. The organization will encounter challenges against which it won't be able to prevail. When evidence of validity can be used to justify and defend the use of measures that produce an adverse impact many organizations nonetheless attempt to apply the adverse impact produced be their assessment methods to extent possible in order to minimize potential interview wrong recuritment decisions and lack of diversity concerns issues to recruit any the most suitable applicants to do any positions in any organizations.

Reference

Barrick, M. R. & Mount , M.K. (1991). The big five personality dimensions and job performance: A meta-analysis, personnel psychology, 91, 1-26.

Costa, P.T. & Jr., & McCrae, R.R. (1992). Four ways five factors are basic. Personality and individual differences, 13, 653-665.

Gottredson, L.S. (Ed). (1982). The g factor in employment, Journal of vacational behavior, 29(3).

Hough, L.. (1992) The big five personality variables construct c confusion: Description versus prediction human performance, 5, 135-155.

Hough, L.M. (1984). Development and evaluation of the " accomplishment record" methods of selecting and promoting professonals. Journal of applied psychology, 69, 135-146.

Hunter, J. (1986). Cognitive ability, cognitive aptitudes, job knowledge and job performance, Journal of vacational behavior, 29, 340-362.

Meichmann, D., Schmitt, N., & Harvey, V.S. (20010. Incremental validity of situatinal judgement tests , Journal of applied psychology, 86, 410-417.

Ree, M.J. Earles, J.A., & Teachout, M.S. (1994), Predicting job performance: Hot much more than g. Journal of applied psychology, 79, 518-524.

Robserton, I. T., & Smith, M. (2001). Personnel Selection. Journal Of Occupational And Organizational Psychological Psychology, 74(4), 441-472.

Sackett, P.R. & Wanek, J.E. (1996). New developments in the use of measures of honesty, integrity, conscientiousness, dependability, trustworthiness and reliability for personnel selection, personnel psychology, 49, 787-829.

Schuler, Randalls, S: Personnel and human resources management. Third edition, 1987.

Shoenfeldt, L.F. (1999). From dustbowl empiricism to rational constructs in biodata. Human resource management review, 9, 147-167.

Steven, Kay Cynthia (1997). Effects of pre-interview beliefs on applicant's reactions to campus interviews. Academy of management journal, 40(4), 947-966.

Stokes, G.S. Mumford, M.D. & owen, W.A. (Eds.) (1994). Biodata handbook paloacto, CA: CPP Books.

Thornton, G.C. III (1992). Assessment centers in human resources management Addison-Wesley,

Whetton, D.A. & Cameron, K.S. (2002). Developing Management , Skill 5th edition, reading, MA: Addison Wesley Longman.

CHAPTER TWO

Developing a successful employee training program steps

To develop one successful employee training program, any employer must need to follow these steps to achieve to train employees to raise efficiencies and improving performance successfully. I recommend these steps to develop one successful training program as below:

The first step: Calculation to every training budget, its needs how much costs to implement. Because designing and arranging one successful training program. It needs expenditure to buy the training course materials, tutors employment and rent office or hotel hall to teach the organizational employees expenditure.

However, training has been proven an important part of continued growth and forward movement for both the employee and the organization as a whole. The organization needs to spend too much money and time to organize any training department programs justified and ensure return on investment. Hence, expenditure budget is needed to evaluate how to spend how much on trainers employment expenditure, courses teaching purchase expenditure, rent office or hotel hall for training teaching expenditure. For example, if the training program needs to spend long time to teach or train employees. It will cause too much training expenditure is needed for long time training period.

So, an absolute training program expenditure budget, e.g. every month, every quarter, every half year, even every year training program budget expenditure. It can avoid actual training expenditure which will exceed budget training expenditure for long time in order to organization's training department.

The second step: Deciding what type of training is needed? Training should be provided before problems or accidents occur. This step is to identify what is needed for people to do their jobs in a safe and productive way. New recruits may need basic training where more experienced workers only need refresher training. To avoid unnecessary training, it is equally important to determine wht kind of training, it is equally important to determine what kind of training is not needed.

The third step: Identifying goals and objectives for your every training program. Clearly stated goals and objectives will identify what your employer to do, to do better, or to stop doing. They don't necessarily have to be written, but in order for the training to be successful, objectives should be thought out before the training begins. Such as when should the training occur? Is it initial training or refresher? Will training include hands-on use of equipment? How much time will be required to training? How will training affect production? Will training be scheduled during work hours or using overtime?

So, when you ensure whether what goals or objectives are for you training program. Then, you will analyze whether you organization is really needed one training program to train your employees or not.

The fourth step: Conducting the training program. Training conducted is needed by professionals will knowledge and expertise in the given subject area is most successful. There are many different methods available to training. It should allow employees to participate in the training process and to practice their skills or knowledge.

The fifth step:Evaluating the effectiveness, testing and evaluating is necessary to measure the success of training. Testing at the ned of training helps determine the amount of learning achieved. providing a training evaluation worksheet following the training program will measure the comfort level and understanding of the training they received. The trainees will also tell the trainers if they feel the trainers are qualified. Also, employees should immediately use the skills they know.

How supervisors observe new and transfer employees to determine of they are doing the job right and they are using the new skills. If the employees don't understand the information they learned in training, they will not use it.

The sixth step: Improving the training program, if after evaluation, it is clear that the necessary to revise the training program. Employers need to ensure every employee has been given the necessary information and training that will enable them to perform their job duties safely. In addition, you might using a different method or facilitator. Asking questions of employees, other training peers and of those who conducted the training may be of some help in improving any of the organization's training programs.

The final step: Designing the suitable type of training. How to design the suitable type of training program, it is very important to train every trainee to achieve their learning aim effectively. The types of training program may include as below:

(1) On -the -job training by peers or group training by management. It's advantages include that questions are easily answered based on experience, trainees are production with less cost and time since training is on-the-job. Trainees hear the same thing from peers working in field. Usually, there is more training time since it is continue.

However it's disadvantges include that trainees learn habits that might be unsafe, there is less control over what traninee's learn, trainees require a good trainer to ensure information is communicated properly and trainees may be rushed and not get adequate training if time is limited. It will influence whose job performance if they can't get adequate training, but they need to do their jobs as the same time.

(2) Next is live instructor lead training by a outside professional. It's advantages include trainees are motivated to learn because of personal attention by outside trainer, the weaknesses or wrong vire points easily identified by professional and are corrected at the time of training, training content is more controlled and objective, job interruptions are limited. So, trainees can focus on training only.

However, it has also disadvantages include that the organization may require a good trainer. He/she may be ill-prepared or unfamiliar with your organization. It could be more costly. The live outside instructor may be difficult to coordinate with other departments and arrangement. The class schedue may be difficult.

(3) Finally, it is electronic instruction on video based/computer assisted training program. It's advantages include that the trainer doesn't need to go to school classroom or workplace or hotel hall or company training room to teach his/ner trainees. He/she can be self directed or self controlled time from video face-to-face computer training channel contact. It is good for annual or refreshed training, virtual environment may be favorable to production , it can be cost effective, due to not need to pay too much

prebooking school classrooms or hotel halls rent for training many employee number every time, e.g. 100 to 1000 trainee number.

In conclusion, all above steps are essential needed to follow to arrange for every training program to any organization. So, trainer must not neglect all any one of these steps if the trainer hope whose training program can be achieved to raise every employee performance and efficiency after they attend the training program.

● What kinds of organizations need training program

I believe innovative organizations need training program to assist whose organizations internal department. What is training and development mean? It means a function of human resource management and it concerns with organizational activity aimed at improving the performance of individuals and groups in organizational strategies. It has been known by human resource development and learning and development.

Why does innovative organization need training program? When an organization is felt that it needs to be innovated, then training and development will be also needed. Training and development is a subsystem of an organization. It ensures that unnecessary repeated or inefficient or unmeaning jobs are reduced and learning or behavioral change takes place in structured format.

So, training and development or learning and development is one of the most important organizations which have better performance or efficiency change to be designed to enhance the fulfillment and performance of employees. So, it brings training and development programs are needed to be offered by a innovative organization might include a variety or educational techniques and programs that can be attened on a compulsory or voluntary basis by staff.

Before any organization's innovation, in general, they never used to believe in training. They were holding the traditional view that managers have responsibilities and effort to do training activities and training is a very costly affair and not worth. But, now the scenario seems to be changed. The modern approach of training and development is that organizations have realized the importance of corporate training. The training industry has been changed to create a smarter workforce and active the best performance improvement and raising efficiency result.

Training and development includes three activities: training, education and development. Training is one activity is both focused upon, and evaluate against, the job that an individual currently holds.

(1) Education is one activity foucuses upon the jobs that an individual may potentially hold in the future, and is evaluated against these jobs.

(2) Development is one activity, focuses upon the activities the organization employing the individual, or that the individual is part of may partake in the future and is almost impossible to evaluate in long term plan.

When an organization is innovated by achieving training program. It will earn these benefits as below:

(1) Discovering or finding employee weaknesses: Most workers have certain weaknesses in their workplace. Training assists in eliminating those weaknesses by strengthening workers skills. A well organized development program helps employees gain similar skills and knowledge ,thus bringing them all to a higher uniform level. It is simply that the whole workforce is reliable, so the whole company or one department doesn't have to rely only on specific employees.

(2) Improvement in workers performance: It is a properly trained employees become more informed about procedures for various tasks needs. The workers confidence is also boostes by training and development. This intangible confidence effort comes from the fact that the employee is fully aeare of his/her role and responsibilities. It helps the worker carry out the duties in better way.

(3) Consistency in duty performance a innovated organization gives the constant knowledge and experience. Consistency is very important when it cases to an change organization's procedures and policies and ethics during execution of duty to all different level of employees from top to down levels.

(4) Raising worker satisfaction: Training and development can drive the great ability to let employees to feel they belong to the company or the organization that they require for and the only way to reward, it is giving the best services they can after they attend any training programs to let they know, and they can judge whether their job degre and effort can achieve to satisfy their organization's demand.

(5) Raising employee individual productivity and improving quality of services: Employees can acquire all the knowledge any one of training program. When they can not learn or feel tasks. Workers can perform at a faster rate and with efficiency thus increasing overall productivity of the company as well as they also gain new duties of overcoming challenges when they face them.

Also, employees can gain standard methods to use in their tasks to maintain uniformity in the output they give. Even reduced cost in supervision, training and development can utilize resources and there is no wastage of resources reducing extra expenses which can caused by accidents occurrence changes during they are working.

Thus, considerately the expected innovative organizations ought choose to set up one training and development department to train trainers to teach trainees in order to raise whose efficiencies and improve performance for whole efficiencies and improve performance for whole organization's innovation aim achievement.

- Reasons of employee training fails and how to solve

In fact, if organizations can not apply corrective ways to facilitate training for employees. It won't improve engagement, productivity and staff retention effectively. The question is why training program can not guarantee any organizations to achieve performance improvement and efficiencies.

The reason is simply. Because these fail training organizations apply wrong training methods, so they can not achieve to improve efficiency and performance under the least budget expenditure spending. The reasons include as below:

(1) The traditional training method is not suitable or still effective to the organization, e.g. it can not help the organization to improve skills, boost morale and build good teams and work processes. I recommend that to maximum the impact of training investment. Organization leader needs to understand how to choose the right training programs, when they need to arrange training and how to select training for the future.

Training must be satisfied to the needs of the organization's staff. The perfect training program ought be excited, interest and engaged the trainees, which encourages them to make use of the training when they need to do their day-to-day jobs to deliver the right training is so important to trainees.

(2) The boring training presentation. Another reason is possible that the trainees feel the training program is bored. It is simply repeat what is being said by the presenter. The audiences feel all the training courses are similar and they are very attractive. So, the training presenter ought consider training time is precious time and organization is paying it, he/she ought not waste organization's precious time to attempt to train whose audiences. So, choosing the right training, it is the trainer's responsibility and he/she must sure that time and money is spent effectively and the

organization must get the best return.

So, choosing what kinds of training fastor which is important to influence whether the training is successful or fail. The different kinds of training may include: 3 D virtual learning and video tuition, face-to-face training, self and paced learning and webiners , e-learning and social learning. For example, e-learning is becoming more popular organizations realize the potential of training staff at their own time and with the least impact to productivity.

It is one kind of skillsoft offer, a wide range of stimulating, engaging and effective learning option. It is different to traditional face-to-dce training. It is exciting, fun internet training tool to let every trainee to talk between them and trainer to discuss any training topic and it can let the trainer explains to them to let they listen and see them clearly by e-learning video tool at home conveniently.

The another training fail reason is that it is important to arrange training that repects that every trainee has different learning styles and rates. Not every trainee is going to want to lead a discussion or be led. A good training course is one that allows everybody to get involved through a range of different methods.

In response to these requirements, skill-soft offers a range of memorable and engaging video-based presentations is the best training to listen the trainer's presentation only, when he/she is watching the video. So, they do not need to discuss and the trainer doesn't need to lead them to listen every online training program. When the trainer arrange the date and time to let all trainees to turn on computer. Then, they can watch the trainer's face and listen whose presentation from onlin video attentively. The trainees will be attractive from the trainer's online training presentation.

This online training method is more better than traditional classroom or workplace training course because a boring class is often the sign of a training provider who has not put enough effort into winning trainees' attention. However, e-learning techniques give mployees access to wider range of trining resources than ever before . They can watch videos, interact with others on the same course and revise topcis at their leisure.

Finally, the training fail reason is that without good planning to a new training program. So, I recommend any one expected training organization nees to consider these factors are related to how to plan good training such as below:

What skills and competencies are required across the training preparation?

Are these skills gaps across the organization?

How to solve these softskills gaps before to achieve one training?
Has the organization developed a training strategy that will ensure training is invested in with the objectives of the company in mind?
Has the organization developed an similar training implementation plan?
How and when will training be delivered?
Can it deliver this training program efficiently, attractively, satisfactory to rais employee productivity efficiencies and improve performance absolutely?
Consequently, I recommend whole organization's top to down level employees who need to participate how to prepare the new training program planning in order to avoid its failure chance. The top level includes executive and senior level managers, the middle level includes middle managers and supervisors and the low level includes the trainers ot the training program. Because training course preparation is whole organization management duty. It is ont only training deparment duty. So, above all these staffs must need to consider how to plan to achieve the training program successfully.

- Prediction rewards and costs of training program

How to calculate every different kinds of training rewards and costs? How to evaluate the training whether it is worth to spend time and time to invest to train employees (trainees)? Whether does the organization need to arrange one training program to let employees (trainees) to be learn new skill knowledge? To answer these question: I shall assume one training program is such as one lotteruy, the lottery buyer will not know whether he/she will win ot lose the lottery, but he/she does not attempt to buy the lottery who won't have chance to win the lucky money.
So, one training program is such one lottery. Whether at the organization as part of a training department of the organization, the training time and money and teaching course material and trainers and training teaching method etc. arrangement must be dominated by the trainer and organization's time. It is determined by their moods. These factors will influence whether the training program can receive rewards or not after it is spent any expenditures are related to the training. Hence, the organization must not know whether how much rewards will be caused by the training program. It only know to plan how much expenditure budget will be spent to the training program. So, training seems to be one lottery game to be played by the player, he/she needs to spend money and time to participate

the lottery game.

Training course is similar to lottery game, the organization needs to spend time and money to arrange trainer and trainees to participate the training program. Hence, whether the worth of training which can earn rewards or not, it needs time to wait. It is hard to predict training reward.

Indeed, economists tend to be unexpectedly indifferent to matters of money, such as cost of every training program. It is a complicating superficial distraction that can usually be assumed away without much harm being (trainer and trainees, employees) done, such as waste or loss of the organization's time and money and human resource to prepare every training program.

It may be natural to look to economics for guidance about earnings, such as future every training program reward. However, when any organization expects to innovate its working environment, office politics, increasing truth, employee royalty, honestry and lies avoidance, raising every high management, middle management and low level working employee individual power and fair promotion, which must need to accept to choose to arrange any suitable training program to satisfy every high management, middle managers and low worker level skills and psychological needs in order to raise their efficiency and productivity and performance effectively. Hence, every organization's innovation aim is similar to playing one lottery game. When the organization can achieve its innovation intention or aim after every different kind of training program.

Then, if it can innovate all its policy, strategy, improving every employee work efficiency and performance, raising productivity etc. different aspects successfully. I believe the organization must earn more reward, due to it has one successful innovation after every different of training to be provided to satisfy all different levels of employee needs from top to low level in the organization.

One open organization is applied one free market principles to time management, such as how it encourages its trainer(s) and trainees (employees) to arrange whose time to participate every different kind of training program efficiently and effectively. So the organization and its trainer(s) and trainee(s) must need time to learn how to arrange time to participate every different kinds of training to avoid to influence their performance or/and productivity efficiency to be worse during they also need time to do their day-to-day job, due to training participation influences their time arrangement spending (opportunity cost) between their

working hours/time and their training participation hours/time.
Thus, arrangement training program time can also give chance to let every trainee(s) and trainer to learn time management issue. Hence, I believe training reward is not only money reward (e.g. profit reward). It includes skill, knowledge upgrade, innovation strategy, policy changing, employee royalty, raising work efficiencies, improving work performance intangible reward. These reward must be the organizstion's future intangible reward. Hence, intangible reward must br more worth to compare tangible reward (profit) because the organization's employees will hav positive emotion or happy mood to serve whose organization if the training program can satisfy all of their psychological needs for long term.
Hence, a small company is arranging only one trainer may have a reasonable reason to require a quick training program decision, but larger firms are playing lottery game to need time spending to decide a training arrangement which is required or not. It is not to their advantage to withdraw the training program offer immediately. They must need spend time to decide whether one training program is required or not.
If they do wrong decision to reject the training program, it is possible to bring future serious economic loss. It can include intangible loss, such as loe efficiency, and low productivity, worse efficiency , waste working time, low employee royalty and bad mood, instead of money (profit) loss. So, large companies must need to spend time to decide whether very training program is worth to be needed to train their employees.

- Can train employees raise efficiency ?

For robot society case, if future our society will be a robot society, based on high technology that high technology can fully replace human beings and workers. Hence, it brings this question: Do any robot manufacturing organizations or applying robot tools to assist productivity organizations need training courses to raise employee individual manufacturing effort to learn how to apply robot tools to assist them to manufacture any products or learn how to manufacture robots to sell ?
Hence, when all artifiacts discovery as well as new technology are created by human intellection. We will achieve outstanding results higher than we expected , such as organization's innovation expectation, if organizations lead and manage correctly their intellection. No one doubts knowledge can manage everything.
Knowledge is a competitive advantage at any level: individual,

organizational and country. In today's more competitive society, employees should learn for better knowledge skills and better performance. So, such as (AI) artificial intelligent industry development cost. I believe every organization must need arrange suitable training programs to raise their employees' efficiencies, productivities and performance by any kinds of (AI) training courses knowledge.

Such as (AI) development case, it proves that employee training of (AI) learning apply knowledge is one of the best ways to accumulate knowledge , use knowledge , update knowledge as well as transfer it to other people in the either (AI) tool applying or (AI) product manufacturing development organization. It is essential to pay more attention to managing the (AI) training knowledge process.

Such as the (AI) development industry, by instilling knowledge is the best way to convert a manual worker into a white collar worker and into a knowledge work, such as one white collar accounting clerk who needs to learn how to apply robot tool to assist he/she raises whose accounting productive efficiency or one vehicle manufacturing worker needs to learn how to apply robot to raise whose efficiency to manufacture any kinds of vehicles for whose employers when their employers accep to adopt robot technology to assist their employees to work to achieve raising productivities and efficiencies aim. So, (AI) training courses may be needed to satisy the employers' innovation needs when they choose to apply (AI) technology to assist their employees to work efficiently to do their day-to-day jobs.

Considerately, training courses skills have the ability to help employees to learn how to manage themselves. The ability of problem solving and decision making, as well as continuing earning consciousness during they need to work with (AI) tools as the same time in every working day in habit. Hence, training courses must have economic worth when the organizations need to apply robots (artificial intelligent tools) (AI) assistanc to raise whose every employee efficiency and productivity and work performance.

Consequently, when society accepts robots technology can be applied to assist any organization's employee to raise whose productivity, efficiency or performance. Then, I believe (AI) training courses will be accepted to be needed to every innovative orgaanization. It proves training can arise intangible and tangible rewards or benefits to every future innovative organization, when they accept (AI) tools assistance to their traditional inefficient worker production method. So, it seems training programs will have it's worth to assist any organization innovation or development to achieve long term benefits.

● Training Super Talent Human Methods

Want a Superior Workforce? How to Develop a High-Performance Workforce ?

A superior workforce is one that is collectively better than an average workforce. It often includes employees who are smarter, faster, more creative, harder working, insightful, aware of the competition, and autonomous. They are daily contributors to a harmonious workplace that emphasizes accountability, reliability, and contribution.

If your goal is a superior, high-performance workforce that is focused on continuous improvement, you need to manage people within a framework that focuses on performance management and development.To achieve this, there are seven components you need to implement. They work together to create a superior, high-performance workforce. Create a checklist to implement these components and to make sure you are following through regularly.

1. Hiring

Create a documented, systematic hiring process. Ensure that you hire the best possible staff for your superior workforce:

· Define the outcomes desired from the people you hire.

· Develop job descriptions that clearly outline the performance responsibilities.

· Develop the largest pool of qualified candidates possible. Search via professional associations, social media networking sites such as LinkedIn, online job boards, personal contacts, employee referrals, university career services offices, search firms, job fairs, newspaper classifieds, and other creative sources when necessary.

· Devise a careful candidate selection process that includes culture match, testing, behavioral interview questions, customer interviews, and tours of the work area.

· Perform appropriate background checks that include employment references, employment history, education, criminal records, credit history, drug testing, and more.

· Make an employment offer that confirms your position as an employer of choice.

2. Defining Goals

Provide the direction and management needed to align the interests of your high-performance workforce with your organization's goals and desired outcomes:

· Provide effective supervisors who give clear direction and expectations, provide frequent feedback, and demonstrate the commitment to staff success.

· Company direction, goals, values, and vision should be communicated frequently and in memorable ways when possible.

· Provide a motivating work environment that helps employees want to come to work every day.

· Provide an empowering, demanding, commitment-oriented work environment with frequent mention of company goals to support your high-performance workforce.

3. Reviewing Progress

Hold quarterly performance development planning (PDPs) meetings to establish aligned direction, measurements, and goals:

· Performance and productivity goals and measurements that support your organization's goals should be developed and written.

· Personal development goals should be agreed upon with individual employees and written. These can range from attendance at a class to cross-training or a new job assignment.

· Most importantly, progress on the performance development goals is tracked for accomplishment. Central tracking by Human Resources ensures the development of the entire workforce.

4. Feedback

Provide regular feedback to employees that lets them know where they stand:

· Effective supervisory feedback means that people know how they are doing daily, via a posted measurement system, verbal or written feedback, and meetings.

· Develop a disciplinary system to help people improve areas in which they are not performing as expected. The system is written, progressive, provides measurements and timelines, and is regularly reviewed with staff members.

5. Employee Recognition

Provide a recognition system that rewards and recognizes people for real contributions:

· Provide equitable pay with a bias toward variable pay using such methods as bonuses and incentives. Whenever possible, pay above market.

· Develop a bonus system that recognizes accomplishments and contributions.

· Design ways to say "thank you" and other employee recognition processes such as company periodic anniversary remembrances, spot awards, team recognition lunches, and more. You are limited only by your imagination.

· Despite the rising cost of health care insurance, which you may need to share with your employees, provide a continually improving benefits package.

6. Training

Provide training, education, and development to build a superior, high-performance workforce:

.Employee retention and education begins with a positive employee orientation. Employee orientation should give new hires a complete understanding of the flow of the business, the nature of the work, employee benefits, and the fit of his or her job within the organization.

· Provide ongoing technical, developmental, managerial, safety, lean manufacturing, and/or workplace organization training and development regularly. The type of training depends on the job. Some experts recommend 40 or more hours of training a year per person.

· Develop a procedure-based, cross-training matrix for each position that includes employee skill testing and periodic, scheduled, on-the-job training and demonstration of capability, for most hands-on jobs.

· Provide regular management and leadership training and coaching from both internal and external sources. The impact of your frontline people on the development of your high-performance workforce is critical.

· Create jobs that enable a staff person to do all the components of a whole task, rather than pieces or parts of a process.

· Develop a learning organization culture through such activities as "lunch and learn," reading books as a team (book club), attending training together, and by making the concept of continuous learning an organization goal.

· Make a commitment to both providing and tracking the accomplishment of the developmental activities promised in the PDPs.

7. Employment Termination

End the employment relationship if the staff person is not working out:

· If you have done your job well—effective orientation, training, clear expectations, coaching, feedback, support—and your new staff person is failing to perform, termination of employment should be swift.

· View every termination as an opportunity for your organization to analyze its hiring, training, integrating, support, and coaching practices and policies. Can you improve any aspect of your process so the next new employee succeeds?

· Perform exit interviews with valued employees who leave. Debrief the same as you would a termination situation.

· Use an employment ending checklist to make certain you have wrapped up all loose ends.

Training method can be applied to employees. Similarity, training method can be also applied to super-athlete sport man.How to Grow a Super-Athlete ? I believe that training must need to grow a super-Athlete. I shall indicate how and why training is needed to grow a tennis super athlete sportman.

The future of tennis training?
A quick analysis of this talent map reveals some splashy numbers: for instance, the average woman in South Korea is more than six times as likely to be a professional golfer as an American woman. But the interesting question is, what underlying dynamic makes these people so spectacularly unaverage in the first place? What force is causing those from certain far-off places to become, competitively speaking, superior?

So even here, at the core of one of the globe's brightest talent blooms, the question of that talent's source remains enigmatically tangled, perhaps as much of a mystery to those who nurture these athletes as it is to the rest of us. It's enough to make you wish for a set of X-ray glasses that could reveal how these invisible forces of culture, history, genes, practice, coaching and belief work together to form that elemental material we call talent — to wish that science could come up with a way to see talent as a substance as tangible as muscle and bone, and whose inner workings we could someday attempt to understand.

However, basketball or tennis sport men, talent is not one main factor cause their super skill raising. Training is one important factor causes their super skill raising. "This is a new dimension that may help us understand a great deal about how the brain works, especially about how we gain skills."

Its very inertness is why the first brain researchers named their new science after the neuron instead of its insulation. They were correct to do so: neurons can indeed explain almost every class of mental phenomenon—memory, emotion, muscle control, sensory perception and so on. But there's one question neurons can't explain: why does it take so long to learn complex skills?

"Everything neurons do, they do pretty quickly; it happens with the flick of a switch," Fields said. "But flicking switches is not how we learn a lot of things. Getting good at piano or chess or baseball takes a lot of time, and that's what myelin is good at."

To the surprise of many neurologists, it turns out this electrical tape is quietly interacting with the neurons. Through a mechanism that Fields and his research team described in a 2006 paper in the journal Neuron, the little sausages of myelin get thicker when the nerve is repeatedly stimulated. The thicker the myelin gets, the better it insulates and the faster and more accurately the signals travel. As Fields puts it, "The signals have to travel at the right speed, arrive at the right time, and myelination is the brain's way of controlling that speed."

"What do good athletes do when they train?" George Bartzokis, a professor of neurology at U.C.L.A., had told me. "They send precise impulses along wires that give the signal to myelinate that wire. They end up, after all the training, with a super-duper wire — lots of bandwidth, high-speed T-1 line. That's what makes them different from the rest of us."

It also left me thinking about the clusters on the talent map. Specifically, wondering whether these places quietly possess myelin-accelerating factors: i.e., forces and conditions that promote what Fields would call "circuit optimization." Might those factors help explain the success of these superior athletes?

Hence, I feel that training is one important factor to manufacture super sport man and super employee. Talent is not the important factor to manufacture super sport man and super employee.

● The talent management skill
raises organizational development
and motivation of employees

When human primitive society is farming primary industry, farmers are only using hand to grow any kinds of plants, vegetable, fruit , rice to sell. Then, the farming work system was organized in primary forms using simple tools and with the least expertise and with division of duties in farm tasks. But in developed farming society, the farming work division is complicated, the farming duties are specialized, and the use of advanced farming technology, such as one farming vehicle can replace farmers' hand to grow any kinds of plants on farms.

The science of growing technology can help any plants to grow in fast speed and kill any animals, they can hurt plants to grow easily. This is good example of human talent technique development in farming industry. It can increase any kinds of plants growing of efficiency in fast speed and short time growing in order to raise plants, fruit food productivies.

If human talent technique can be applied to our business society. Can human talent technique help any organization job characteristics raising efficiency and intrinsic motivation is more for the employees that are satisfied with their growth, and the employees with more experience were more satisfied with supervisor and collegues.

How can organizations apply talent management technique to raise work quality of the employees and their attempts? If any organizations hope to raise employee motivation. They need to concern how to change any job forms of content, job process to be more attractive. In order to achieve employees motivation more efficiently. For example, if the organization's employees can be motivated by more payments, fewer work hours, and suitable work condition. This kind of organizational talent management method ought bring employees motivation can be increased through providing independence and responsibility of the employees. The question concerns: Which factor or which factors motivate each employee in any organizations? Because every organization has different characteristics and different job title and duty. Some every organization factors motivate employees, they ought be different. Every organization ought focus on why individuals choose certain behavioral alternatives for satisfaction of needs in order to seek what factor(s) can increase its employees' motivation. Hence, if the organization has high degree of job motivation and satisfaction. The organization can predict the organizational commitment positively. So, it seems that one high degree of job motivation an satisfactory organization can bring high employee productivities turnover.

Organizational strategic talent method aims to create an accessible source of talents for adapting the right individuals with the right jobs and the right time based on the strategic purposes of business. Because the lack of talent is the biggest obstacle on the lack is a kind of major strategic advantage. Hence, any organization managers must need to know how to manage talents. How to use the individuals and how strategically to place them in proper position. Managers must design the situation to have the maximum knowledge and information, innovation and effort. And identify and discover whom are talents scarce and underdeveloped resources, how to seek talented employees. Such as talent labor market, it has key factors influence the efficiency of entering the labor market. These factors are the analysis of the current labor market situation and the rational preference of specialization. The active search and the talent employees interviewing, talent employees labor market search, these components are any organizations' talent recruitment essential method, if they hope to recurit any talented people to serve their organizations absolutely. Instead of talent recruitment factor, the other factors influence organizational success. They may include: Whether the organization has implemented feedback surveys, sensitivity training, management network, practical research, and training the techniques of improvement of intrapersonal relationships. So, those soft skills will be any successful organizations' essential talent management methods. So, organizations can not neglect any one of these factors in order to employee talented people to serve their organizations effectively.

● What is strategic talent management skill?

Strategic talent management skill can maximize the competitive advantage of an organization's human capital, this talent management is even more significant to be needed in nowadays organizational management, e.g. how to develop a talent pool of high potential and high performance to fill the organizatons' any roles as well as how to develop in differentiated human resource strategy to facilitate filling these positions with competent and to ensure all employees are talent to continue commitment to the organizations.

It is important to note that key positions are not necessarily restricted to the top management team (TMT), but also include key positions at levels lower than the TME and many vary between operating units and time. The reason is because any organization ought not need a stable top position, and this top position ought may be variable any time.

For one bank organization example, it ought not only CEO top position. It ought follow its market need to change CEO position, e.g. sometimes the bank may have more than one CEO position, e.g. share selling division CEO, housing loan division CEO, investment division CEO. Moreover, the lower position , such as manager can also increase to two or more, e.g. house loan division can have one CEO manager two housing loan department managers, even more. If the house loan division needs to increase staffs number to do any loan administration, loan applicaion and loan confirmation tasks in the house loan clients number busy time. So, bank top management CEO and lower management manager positions number can not ought keep only one. It is one wrong talent management strategy. It ought follow the client number to decide how to increase the right employees number in order to decide whether the bank's any department ought employ one CEO or manager position or more in order to solve the bank clients need number. Because if the bank only have one CEO and manager to manage their department. They will feel difficulty, if employees and bank clients number are increasing suddenly. They will feel busy and feel stressful. So, the bank ought need to decide whether the only one CEO and one manager to every department in busy time. It is suitable to its any departments to cooperate efficiently. Because if its any one department's management is inefficient, then it will influence employee performance and client dissatisfaction. So, the bank talent management method is that any time changes CEO and manager number to any department. Hence, organizational talent management depends on employees, clients number , market need, labor market supply factors.

- Talent in the world of work meaning

Talent in the world of work concerns talent management , high performers, high potentials and talent workforce segmentation. Talent should refer to a person's recurring patterns of thought, feeling or behavior that can be productivity applied. The sum of a person's abilities, his or her intrinsic gifts, skills, knowledge, experience, intelligence, judgement, attitudes, character and drive. Talent can be considered as a complex employees‘ skills, knowledge, cognitive ability and potential. Employees' values and work preferences are also of major importance, a select group of employees, those that rank at the top in terms of capability and preference, rather than the job, times commitment, willing to do the job, times contribition finding meaning and purpose in their work.

Hence, a talent person or worker who ensures the competitiveness, and future of a company as specialist or leader, through his organizational job specific qualification and knowledge , his social and methodical competencies, ans his characteristic attributes , such as eager to learn or achievement oriented. A talent person or worker has these characteristics: competence, knowledge, skills and values required for today' and tomorrow's job, right skills, right place, right job, right time and contribution , finding meaning and any nowadays talent person's characteristics.

Does talent refers to people (subject) or to the characteristics of people (object) ? Is talent more about performance, potential , competence, or commitment? Is talent a natural ability or does it relates more to further improving through practice? Talent is typically associated with athletes (e.g. Olympians, exceptional coaches, extraordinary teams, musicians of extraordinary ability, singers with incredible voices). It is commonly understood as above-average ability for a specific function or range or functions. Rather than corresponding to " normal" ability, talent is considered a special ability that makes the people who posses, develop and use it in the specific area of their talent.

Consequently, talent is often meant to excellent performance in a given performance domain. But in working society, talent has another meaning, i.e. people posses special skills or abilities. For job advertisement in which talent refers to potential applicants (e.g. talent wanted).

Talent s as a kind of natural ability, more than training to own personal skills capacity. In general, talent person owns a unique mix of innate intelligence or brain power, and a certain degree of creativity or the capacity to go beyond estabished stereotypes and provide innovative solutions to problems in his everyday life more easily to compare common people.

In general, common people or student or worker can be taught to own skills and knowledge to learn easily. But , talent has characteristics much more unique. Therefore, talent is impossible to learn or teach easily. It is the person innate nature owns, talent can not really managed by any persons or organizations easily, because talent is always a function of experience and effort, e.g. an excellent sport person can be trained to be one excellent sport skillful talent person, even he has not one talent sport skillful person to any kinds of sport, e.g. riding bicycle, sport. If the sport person is not excellent in riding bicycle sport, but if he has a good trainer, he can teach good riding bicycle method or skill to be trained him to be one riding bicycle sporter. Then, for a long time riding bicycle learning perios, he will have possible to be one talent riding bicycle sport person. So, in some situaton, one non-talent learner will be trained to be one talent learner, if the trainer has good skills and methods to teach the trainee, such as riding bicycle sport case, it is not all riding bicycle sport person is one talent sport man. Their excellent riding bicycle skills need to be trained to raise their riding bicycle skills. Then, their talent on riding bicycle skills will be raised to be performed in possible. So, for sport man case, talent is not natural, talent sport man (trainee) is trained by trainer.

Hence, creating a talent person, it depends on these factors: The right place, the right position, and/or the right time. Such as the riding bicycle sport trainee case, he needs have right riding bicycle learning school , e.g. riding bicycle facility, good quality bicycle and large bicycle indoor spor place to let the bicycle sport trainee to learn. Then, he also needs a good trainee to learn. Then, he also needs a good bicycle teaching trainer , he can teach good riding bicycle skill and fast speed riding and safe riding knowledge to let him to ride his bicycle in the riding bicycle competitive games in the

fastest speed safely in order to win his riding bicycle competitors.
Finally, right time is also important factor, if in the time, the riding bicycle trainee has physical body hurt challenge or poor emotion psychological challenge. These factors will influnce his riding bicycle learning performance or abilities in order to achieve the best performance level. So, he needs to wait the time, he has good physical health and good emotion psychological time, then he can learn his riding bicycle trainer's riding bicycle knowledge and skill easily. Hence, one talent sport man needs have above these thress basic requirements: right place, right position, right ime in order to achieve the talent sport man training in success.

CHAPTER THREE

Training Super Talent Human Methods

● Non-training method creates talent young people

Want a Superior Workforce? How to Develop a High-Performance Workforce ?

A superior workforce is one that is collectively better than an average workforce. It often includes employees who are smarter, faster, more creative, harder working, insightful, aware of the competition, and autonomous. They are daily contributors to a harmonious workplace that emphasizes accountability, reliability, and contribution.

If your goal is a superior, high-performance workforce that is focused on continuous improvement, you need to manage people within a framework that focuses on performance management and development.To achieve this, there are seven components you need to implement. They work together to create a superior, high-performance workforce. Create a checklist to implement these components and to make sure you are following through regularly.

1. Hiring

Create a documented, systematic hiring process. Ensure that you hire the best possible staff for your superior workforce:

· Define the outcomes desired from the people you hire.

· Develop job descriptions that clearly outline the performance responsibilities.

· Develop the largest pool of qualified candidates possible. Search via professional associations, social media networking sites such as LinkedIn, online job boards, personal contacts, employee referrals, university career services offices, search firms, job fairs, newspaper classifieds, and other creative sources when necessary.

· Devise a careful candidate selection process that includes culture match, testing, behavioral interview questions, customer interviews, and tours of the work area.

· Perform appropriate background checks that include employment references, employment history, education, criminal records, credit history, drug testing, and more.

· Make an employment offer that confirms your position as an employer of choice.

2. Defining Goals

Provide the direction and management needed to align the interests of your high-performance workforce with your organization's goals and desired outcomes:

· Provide effective supervisors who give clear direction and expectations, provide frequent feedback, and demonstrate the commitment to staff success.

· Company direction, goals, values, and vision should be communicated frequently and in memorable ways when possible.

· Provide a motivating work environment that helps employees want to come to work every day.

· Provide an empowering, demanding, commitment-oriented work environment with frequent mention of company goals to support your high-performance workforce.

3. Reviewing Progress

Hold quarterly performance development planning (PDPs) meetings to establish aligned direction, measurements, and goals:

· Performance and productivity goals and measurements that support your organization's goals should be developed and written.

· Personal development goals should be agreed upon with individual employees and written. These can range from attendance at a class to cross-training or a new job assignment.

· Most importantly, progress on the performance development goals is tracked for accomplishment. Central tracking by Human Resources ensures the development of the entire workforce.

4. Feedback

Provide regular feedback to employees that lets them know where they stand:

· Effective supervisory feedback means that people know how they are doing daily, via a posted measurement system, verbal or written feedback, and meetings.

· Develop a disciplinary system to help people improve areas in which they are not performing as expected. The system is written, progressive, provides measurements and timelines, and is regularly reviewed with staff members.

5. Employee Recognition

Provide a recognition system that rewards and recognizes people for real contributions:

· Provide equitable pay with a bias toward variable pay using such methods as bonuses and incentives. Whenever possible, pay above market.

· Develop a bonus system that recognizes accomplishments and contributions.

· Design ways to say "thank you" and other employee recognition processes such as company periodic anniversary remembrances, spot awards, team recognition lunches, and more. You are limited only by your imagination.

· Despite the rising cost of health care insurance, which you may need to share with your employees, provide a continually improving benefits package.

6. Training

Provide training, education, and development to build a superior, high-performance workforce:

.Employee retention and education begins with a positive employee orientation. Employee orientation should give new hires a complete understanding of the flow of the business, the nature of the work, employee benefits, and the fit of his or her job within the organization.

· Provide ongoing technical, developmental, managerial, safety, lean manufacturing, and/or workplace organization training and development regularly. The type of training depends on the job. Some experts recommend 40 or more hours of training a year per person.

· Develop a procedure-based, cross-training matrix for each position that includes employee skill testing and periodic, scheduled, on-the-job training and demonstration of capability, for most hands-on jobs.

· Provide regular management and leadership training and coaching from both internal and external sources. The impact of your frontline people on the development of your high-performance workforce is critical.

· Create jobs that enable a staff person to do all the components of a whole task, rather than pieces or parts of a process.

· Develop a learning organization culture through such activities as "lunch and learn," reading books as a team (book club), attending training together, and by making the concept of continuous learning an organization goal.

· Make a commitment to both providing and tracking the accomplishment of the developmental activities promised in the PDPs.

7. Employment Termination

End the employment relationship if the staff person is not working out:

· If you have done your job well—effective orientation, training, clear expectations, coaching, feedback, support—and your new staff person is failing to perform, termination of employment should be swift.

· View every termination as an opportunity for your organization to analyze its hiring, training, integrating, support, and coaching practices and policies. Can you improve any aspect of your process so the next new employee succeeds?

· Perform exit interviews with valued employees who leave. Debrief the same as you would a termination situation.

· Use an employment ending checklist to make certain you have wrapped up all loose ends.

Training method can be applied to employees. Similarity, training method can be also applied to super-athlete sport man.How to Grow a Super-Athlete ? I believe that training must need to grow a super-Athlete. I shall indicate how and why training is needed to grow a tennis super athlete sportman.

The future of tennis training?

A quick analysis of this talent map reveals some splashy numbers: for instance, the average woman in South Korea is more than six times as likely to be a professional golfer as an American woman. But the interesting question is, what underlying dynamic makes these people so spectacularly unaverage in the first place? What force is causing those from certain far-off places to become, competitively speaking, superior?

So even here, at the core of one of the globe's brightest talent blooms, the question of that talent's source remains enigmatically tangled, perhaps as much of a mystery to those who nurture these athletes as it is to the rest of us. It's enough to make you wish for a set of X-ray glasses that could reveal how these invisible forces of culture, history, genes, practice, coaching and belief work together to form that elemental material we call talent — to wish that science could come up with a way to see talent as a substance as tangible as muscle and bone, and whose inner workings we could someday attempt to understand.

However, basketball or tennis sport men, talent is not one main factor cause their super skill raising. Training is one important factor causes their super skill raising. "This is a new dimension that may help us understand a great deal about how the brain works, especially about how we gain skills."

Its very inertness is why the first brain researchers named their new science after the neuron instead of its insulation. They were correct to do so: neurons can indeed explain almost every class of mental phenomenon—memory, emotion, muscle control, sensory perception and so on. But there's one question neurons can't explain: why does it take so long to learn complex skills?

"Everything neurons do, they do pretty quickly; it happens with the flick of a switch," Fields said. "But flicking switches is not how we learn a lot of things. Getting good at piano or chess or baseball takes a lot of time, and that's what myelin is good at."

To the surprise of many neurologists, it turns out this electrical tape is quietly interacting with the neurons. Through a mechanism that Fields and his research team described in a 2006 paper in the journal Neuron, the little sausages of myelin get thicker when the nerve is repeatedly stimulated. The thicker the myelin gets, the better it insulates and the faster and more accurately the signals travel. As Fields puts it, "The signals have to travel at the right speed, arrive at the right time, and myelination is the brain's way of controlling that speed."

"What do good athletes do when they train?" George Bartzokis, a professor of neurology at U.C.L.A., had told me. "They send precise impulses along wires that give the signal to myelinate that wire. They end up, after all the training, with a super-duper wire — lots of bandwidth, high-speed T-1 line. That's what makes them different from the rest of us."

It also left me thinking about the clusters on the talent map. Specifically, wondering whether these places quietly possess myelin-accelerating factors: i.e., forces and conditions that promote what Fields would call "circuit optimization." Might those factors help explain the success of these superior athletes?
Hence, I feel that training is one important factor to manufacture super sport man and super employee. Talent is not the important factor to manufacture super sport man and super employee.

● The talent management skill
raises organizational development
and motivation of employees

When human primitive society is farming primary industry, farmers are only using hand to grow any kinds of plants, vegetable, fruit , rice to sell. Then, the farming work system was organized in primary forms using simple tools and with the least expertise and with division of duties in farm tasks. But in developed farming society, the farming work division is complicated, the farming duties are specialized, and the use of advanced farming technology, such as one farming vehicle can replace farmers' hand to grow any kinds of plants on farms.

The science of growing technology can help any plants to grow in fast speed and kill any animals, they can hurt plants to grow easily. This is good example of human talent technique development in farming industry. It can increase any kinds of plants growing of efficiency in fast speed and short time growing in order to raise plants, fruit food productivies.

If human talent technique can be applied to our business society. Can human talent technique help any organization job characteristics raising efficiency and intrinsic motivation is more for the employees that are satisfied with their growth, and the employees with more experience were more satisfied with supervisor and collegues.

How can organizations apply talent management technique to raise work quality of the employees and their attempts? If any organizations hope to raise employee motivation. They need to concern how to change any job forms of content, job process to be more attractive. In order to achieve employees motivation more efficiently. For example, if the organization's employees can be motivated by more payments, fewer work hours, and suitable work condition. This kind of organizational talent management method ought bring employees motivation can be increased through providing independence and responsibility of the employees. The question concerns: Which factor or which factors motivate each employee in any organizations? Because every organization has different characteristics and different job title and duty. Some every organization factors motivate employees, they ought be different. Every organization ought focus on why individuals choose certain behavioral alternatives for satisfaction of needs in order to seek what factor(s) can increase its employees' motivation. Hence, if the organization has high degree of job motivation and satisfaction. The organization can predict the organizational commitment positively. So, it seems that one high degree of job motivation an satisfactory organization can bring high employee productivities turnover.

Organizational strategic talent method aims to create an accessible source of talents for adapting the right individuals with the right jobs and the right time based on the strategic purposes of business. Because the lack of talent is the biggest obstacle on the lack is a kind of major strategic advantage. Hence, any organization managers must need to know how to manage talents. How to use the individuals and how strategically to place them in proper position. Managers must design the situation to have the maximum knowledge and information, innovation and effort. And identify and discover whom are talents scarce and underdeveloped resources, how to seek talented employees. Such as talent labor market, it has key factors influence the efficiency of entering the labor market. These factors are the analysis of the current labor market situation and the rational preference of specialization. The active search and the talent employees interviewing, talent employees labor market search, these components are any organizations' talent recruitment essential method, if they hope to recurit any talented people to serve their organizations absolutely. Instead of talent recruitment factor, the other factors influence organizational success. They may include: Whether the organization has implemented feedback surveys, sensitivity training, management network, practical research, and training the techniques of improvement of intrapersonal relationships. So, those soft skills will be any successful organizations' essential talent management methods. So, organizations can not neglect any one of these factors in order to employee talented people to serve their organizations effectively.

● What is strategic talent management skill?

Strategic talent management skill can maximize the competitive advantage of an organization's human capital, this talent management is even more significant to be needed in nowadays organizational management, e.g. how to develop a talent pool of high potential and high performance to fill the organizatons' any roles as well as how to develop in differentiated human resource strategy to facilitate filling these positions with competent and to ensure all employees are talent to continue commitment to the organizations.

It is important to note that key positions are not necessarily restricted to the top management team (TMT), but also include key positions at levels lower than the TME and many vary between operating units and time. The reason is because any organization ought not need a stable top position, and this top position ought may be variable any time.

For one bank organization example, it ought not only CEO top position. It ought follow its market need to change CEO position, e.g. sometimes the bank may have more than one CEO position, e.g. share selling division CEO, housing loan division CEO, investment division CEO. Moreover, the lower position , such as manager can also increase to two or more, e.g. house loan division can have one CEO manager two housing loan department managers, even more. If the house loan division needs to increase staffs number to do any loan administration, loan applicaion and loan confirmation tasks in the house loan clients number busy time. So, bank top management CEO and lower management manager positions number can not ought keep only one. It is one wrong talent management strategy. It ought follow the client number to decide how to increase the right employees number in order to decide whether the bank's any department ought employ one CEO or manager position or more in order to solve the bank clients need number. Because if the bank only have one CEO and manager to manage their department. They will feel difficulty, if employees and bank clients number are increasing suddenly. They will feel busy and feel stressful. So, the bank ought need to decide whether the only one CEO and one manager to every department in busy time. It is suitable to its any departments to cooperate efficiently. Because if its any one department's management is inefficient, then it will influence employee performance and client dissatisfaction. So, the bank talent management method is that any time changes CEO and manager number to any department. Hence, organizational talent management depends on employees, clients number , market need, labor market supply factors.

● Talent in the world of work meaning

Talent in the world of work concerns talent management , high performers, high potentials and talent workforce segmentation. Talent should refer to a person's recurring patterns of thought, feeling or behavior that can be productivity applied. The sum of a person's abilities, his or her intrinsic gifts, skills, knowledge, experience, intelligence, judgement, attitudes, character and drive. Talent can be considered as a complex employees' skills, knowledge, cognitive ability and potential. Employees' values and work preferences are also of major importance, a select group of employees, those that rank at the top in terms of capability and preference, rather than the job, times commitment, willing to do the job, times contribition finding meaning and purpose in their work.

Hence, a talent person or worker who ensures the competitiveness, and future of a company as specialist or leader, through his organizational job specific qualification and knowledge , his social and methodical competencies, ans his characteristic attributes , such as eager to learn or achievement oriented. A talent person or worker has these characteristics: competence, knowledge, skills and values required for today' and tomorrow's job, right skills, right place, right job, right time and contribution , finding meaning and any nowadays talent person's characteristics.

Does talent refers to people (subject) or to the characteristics of people (object) ? Is talent more about performance, potential , competence, or commitment? Is talent a natural ability or does it relates more to further improving through practice? Talent is typically associated with athletes (e.g. Olympians, exceptional coaches, extraordinary teams, musicians of extraordinary ability, singers with incredible voices). It is commonly understood as above-average ability for a specific function or range or functions. Rather than corresponding to " normal" ability, talent is considered a special ability that makes the people who posses, develop and use it in the specific area of their talent.

Consequently, talent is often meant to excellent performance in a given performance domain. But in working society, talent has another meaning, i.e. people posses special skills or abilities. For job advertisement in which talent refers to potential applicants (e.g. talent wanted).

Talent s as a kind of natural ability, more than training to own personal skills capacity. In general, talent person owns a unique mix of innate intelligence or brain power, and a certain degree of creativity or the capacity to go beyond estabished stereotypes and provide innovative solutions to problems in his everyday life more easily to compare common people.

In general, common people or student or worker can be taught to own skills and knowledge to learn easily. But , talent has characteristics much more unique. Therefore, talent is impossible to learn or teach easily. It is the person innate nature owns, talent can not really managed by any persons or organizations easily, because talent is always a function of experience and effort, e.g. an excellent sport person can be trained to be one excellent sport skillful talent person, even he has not one talent sport skillful person to any kinds of sport, e.g. riding bicycle, sport. If the sport person is not excellent in riding bicycle sport, but if he has a good trainer, he can teach good riding bicycle method or skill to be trained him to be one riding bicycle sporter. Then, for a long time riding bicycle learning perios, he will have possible to be one talent riding bicycle sport person. So, in some situaton, one non-talent learner will be trained to be one talent learner, if the trainer has good skills and methods to teach the trainee, such as riding bicycle sport case, it is not all riding bicycle sport person is one talent sport man. Their excellent riding bicycle skills need to be trained to raise their riding bicycle skills.

Then, their talent on riding bicycle skills will be raised to be performed in possible. So, for sport man case, talent is not natural, talent sport man (trainee) is trained by trainer.

Hence, creating a talent person, it depends on these factors: The right place, the right position, and/or the right time. Such as the riding bicycle sport trainee case, he needs have right riding bicycle learning school , e.g. riding bicycle facility, good quality bicycle and large bicycle indoor spor place to let the bicycle sport trainee to learn. Then, he also needs a good trainee to learn. Then, he also needs a good bicycle teaching trainer , he can teach good riding bicycle skill and fast speed riding and safe riding knowledge to let him to ride his bicycle in the riding bicycle competitive games in the fastest speed safely in order to win his riding bicycle competitors.

Finally, right time is also important factor, if in the time, the riding bicycle trainee has physical body hurt challenge or poor emotion psychological challenge. These factors will influnce his riding bicycle learning performance or abilities in order to achieve the best performance level. So, he needs to wait the time, he has good physical health and good emotion psychological time, then he can learn his riding bicycle trainer's riding bicycle knowledge and skill easily. Hence, one talent sport man needs have above these thress basic requirements: right place, right position, right ime in order to achieve the talent sport man training in success.

● Building high performance culture
talent management method
to organizations

Any human decision making can influence our organizations value. How our culture causes may influence how we can fall serve to our organization? Our organization culture can influence how we bring energy, creativity and enthusiasm to our organization value. So, it brings these questions concern how our organizational culture can bring high performance to our organization productivity , such as:

How can our talent management to our organization culture can bring consequence on increasing profits and shareholder value, attracting and keeping talented people, building brand loyalty, ensure that ethic corporate culture to achieve high performance. Also, how out talent management to our organization culture can help we deliver high quality , cost effective services and a sustainable society service. The key questions concern how building a high performance culture to our private and public sector organizations. We need to know that the culture of an private organization's source comes from its competitive advantage and brand differentiation, as well as the culture of an public organization source comes from its cost effectiveness and quality of services.

Hence one successful public and private organization cultures may bring these performance effects: values and behaviors drive cutlure, culture drives employee fulfilment, employee fulfilment drives customer satisfaction and mission achievement. Because any organizational staff's cultural behavior, their principles, ideas, or briefs that people (staffs) can influence organizational operation. For example, similarly, if the organization has potentially limiting value of bureaucracy, that it can cause rigidity and limit the free idea expression from any staffs. This organization cultural value will limit employees‘ personal value and poor financial peformance because it's organizational cultural value is not " open mind" or let employees have chance to share their opinions to discuss their company any issues very easily.

So, bureaucracy cultural value will be weakness to any organizations, e.g. some countries' government organization is bureaucracy cultural value. It can not innovate or raise or improve its government internal organization different departments‘ efficiencies very easily. But, it needs lone time to do any decisions . It is a bureaucracy organization's weakness or easy cooperation between the values of the culture of the organization and the personal values of employees, the final effect is low performance, which can further resultin low levels of staff engagement and poor quality of products and services. All these bureacucracy organization's long time decision making and messages need long time delivery factors can have a significant impact on the financial performance or low efficiency (inefficiency) of the organization or its ability to deliver services of low quality.

Hence, if the organization's culture is able to attract and retain talented individuals. This gives organizations a significant commercial advantage, especially when talent is in short supply. Strong brand values are always those with the strongest internal cultures. So, it has relationship between high cultures, brand differentiation, or retaining talented individuals and the successful is highly dependent on the culture that the leaders create.

Also, the culture that leaders create is highly dependent on the behaviors of the leaders and their relationship to other leaders in the organization, and their relationships with their employees. It explains that why organizations with strong , high performing cultures tend to replace their leaders by promoting from within, whereas low -performing cultures tend to replace their leader's with external candidates. The reason is because that by promoting from within, organization's good cultures are also to retain their successful leadership styles. However, organization's culture and desired leadership styles is one kind of management feeling from all employees and managers working behavior and attitude. Any organizations must need spend time to research what their organization culture is and what leaders desired leadership styles are.

How can we know our organization culture is suitable to let our low level and high level employees accept to work together? We can follow those change to judge whether our organization's culture is suitable organization culture. The change may include: A different way of doing. Doing what we do now, but doing it in a more efficient, productive, or quality -enhancing way, a different way of being. Transformation involves changes at the deepest levels of beliefs, values and assumptions. Transformation occurs when we are also be learnt from our mistakes, are open to a new future, and can let revise of the part mistakes.

Hence talent retension is critically important for all organizations for two main reasons: Turnover is expensive and top performers drive business performance. Turnover costs arise from the direct replacement costs of talent acquisition, the opportunity costs of vacant positions and time to productivity, in the result costing of business performance. Hence, one organization has good cultural value, it may have characteristics: The organization can have confidence to recruit the right people in the first place, it can improve the line manager's ability to manage, it can give employee's constrant feedback about clear, meaningful goals, it can empower employees to manage their own careers, it can continuously measure and improve retention strategies easily. All of these are any good cultural organization's characteristics.

Hence, talent managemen may a key aspect of human resources management strategy in any organizations? In this age of the rapily expanding knowledge-based economy, the quality of human resources has assumed crucial importance. This complex and demanding market environment has a demand for outstanding and talented with high development potential, being the lever of growth in shareholder value. The organization talent leader has attitude, a performance -oriented approach, the ability to persuade, teamwork, emotional intelligence, flexibility, a high tolerance to change, and highly developed specialist technical skills.

However, it has relationship between developing talent people and good organizational culture. Because developing talent people and good culture, then it can develop talent people easily.
How can we know that the organization has good culture. Similarly, if we discover that the organization has many talent people are working, then we may assume that the organization has good organizational culture . We can follow how many employees' talent level, they own and they are working in the organization. The talent level can consist of these several points: Extraordinary intellectual skills (general and specialist), a creative attitude (originality, flexible thinking and acting, solving unconventional problems easily, and a high tolerance to risk, change , uncertainty) and a commitment to work (self-disciplined, persistent in pursuing goals, and hard-working). Hence, if the organization has many employees, who own extraordinary intellectual skills, a creative attitude, a commitment to work attitude. Then, I believe that the organization owns many talent suitable to let them to feel to work.
Hence, what is talent management cultural organization? A talent management cultural organization can ensure that talent people are attracted, retained, motivated and developed in line with the needs of the organization, i.e. the most valuable staff memebers, by creating conditions conducive to their potential development. So that they can be put to use for the company's operations for as long as possible, talent management is a set of activities taken vis-a vis personnel with outstanding talents to ensure their development and increase their operational efficiency, when immediately achieve corporate goals easily. A talent management cultural organization consists of searching for talents inside or outside the organization, undertaking special activities to enable their development, training and career path planning and ensuring that their remuneration is competitive with that of other organizations, talent management involves implementing a set of key activities as part od human resource management , when immediately applying more advanced methods and techniques.
Hence, one talent management cultural organization ought own above all these characteristics. A talent management cultural organization can reduce employee turnover number, they can keep talent people continue stay to work in their organization for long time. So, when the organization's workforce (employee leaving) turnove rate reduces, in special talent employees, then its high performers and employees with hard-to-replace skills, these group employees will continue work in their present employers

for long time.

Similarly, any talent management cultural organization really can prove itself is one successful organization , it must need long time to learn or improve itself strategy in order to attract many talent employees choose itself organization to work. Hence," learning how to attract talent employee method", which is a important factor to influence whether the organization can be one talent management cultural organization in success.

How can a digital platform one online talent platform assist organizations to recruit talent people? Online talent platforms can ease a number of these dysfunctions by more effective connecting individuals with work opportunities. Labor markets are arriving in the form of digital platforms, the very same technologies that have reshaped the businesses and consumer environment in areas , such as e-commerce.

Online talent platforms are marketplaces and tools that can connect individuals to the right work opportunities. The size of their user networks expand the pool of possibilities, and their powerful search capabilities in an efficient and personalized way. These digital platforms are rapidly popular, acceptable to apply on online talent recruitment method for any organizations.

Talent online recuritment platforms can help companies transform or change the traditional recruitment way or method. They hire, train and manage their employees. All this online talent recruitment method can give better-informed decisions about human capital produce better business results. In additions, online talent recruitment platform could improve signaling about the skill that are actually in demand across the economy. As this information shapes decisions about education and training, the entire skills mix of the economy could adjust more accurately over time.

Online talent recruitment platforms can take form of websites mobile apps, or proprietary corporate systems. They gather a huge volume of information regarding both individual workers and employers or work projects, then synthesize this data to match individuals with job opportunities and produce better work outcomes.

One online talent recruitment platform is a digital tools that enable users (organizations) to post full time or part time jobs, create online resumes of individuals, search for talent or work opportunities, based on extended matching attributes, provide personal working experience and qualification data into company or worker reputations, skills, assess candidates' attributes, skills or fit, personalize onboarding, training and talent

management optimize team formation and internal matching, determine the best options for training and skill development.
Hence, online recruitment talent management platform will be a good tool to any organizations' human resource department talent employee choice method to help them to select the most talent employee(s) to work in the right position and in right time. It can replace the traditional newspapers applicant recruitment method or outsoucing job agent applicant recuriment method or government labor department post recruitment method. When one organization has many employees, e.g. 100, even 1000, 10000 or more employees number. Online talent recruitment platform can help it to reduce to spend much time to choose whom are the right applicatns to apply the job position, because (artificial intelligence) AI technology can replace human's judgement ability, it's judgement accurate level may exceed to human judgement level to choose the right applicants to enter the next interview stage. So, it explains that why online talent recruitment platform can replace any organization's human resource department's CV sceening process. It is one good (AI) online recruitment platform to help any recruiters' CV sceening process to be avoided, when (AI) online recruitment CV screening platform method is invented to assist any large organizations' human resource department to reduce time and staff nervous to do every applicant's CV screening activity. This is one good talent management application and recruitment and selection method to any large organizations' large human resource recruitment process.

Among young people are potential philosophers, artists, writers, entrepreneurs, whether training method is one important factor to create or manufacture any one of young peole to be super talent person successfully in our society. Some psychologists or behavioral scientists or doctors believe that formal educational (school) training is only the important method to train super talent young people. But, other some psychologists or behavioral scientists or doctors , they argue that formal educaiton (school) training is not the main method to create any one super talent young person in our society.Otherwise, they also feel that non-formal educaiotn method will be easily to create or manufacture one real super talent person in our society nowadays.

I agree the later professional groups' view point any more. I believe that the young person himself/herself free learning
atitude factor is the most influential method to attract any one capacity

within the young person to be one super talent person in society in possible more. The super talent young people can discover or seek whether what the real capability, they own

in success. They have these same characteristics: They can spend time to attempt to seek whether what their talent capability may own in order

to develop their talent capabilities. Moreover, they do not need any teachers to teach how they may discover their talent capabilities in success in classrooms. Otherwise, they accept to spend their extra non-schooling time to seek whether what kind of talent capabilities , they may own in habit. Because when they feel what kind of talent capabilities that they may own in possible, then they will have habitual behaviors to be creative and innovative to their specialized talent undiscovered capabiliities often. Due to their accumulative time creates and innovates and concentrate on learning their one kind of talent capability, then they can enhance their the ability of non-formal education learning experience method to create or upgrade or raise the kind of their talent capabilities easily.

The question concerns: How do these common young people not need training method to create or innovate or raise

their talent capabilities to become one super talent young person in success? In fact, any one super talent person, he/she

must be common person in past long time before. It depends on whe he/she can discover or seek whether what the real talent capability that he/she may own in order to upgrade or raise himself/herself this kind of talent capability in success. Even, when he/she knows or ensures that this kind of talent capability , he/she has owned really. He/she also needs long time to learn in order to upgrade or raise this kind of talent capability. SO, any one super talent young person must need long time to learn the kind of capability in order to be the kind of capability super talent young person.

Hence, it explains why school formal educaiton can not train any super talent students focus on one kind of capability in success. Schools can only provide one group students classroom learning environment to train any one common lazy student to be hard student to attempt to earn high grade to each subject in order to graduate to seek any kinds of occupation in achievement in our society. Otherwise, any one super talent owning one kind of capability at least person, who will not need school learning training method.

They need to spend time to discover any one kind of talent capability , that they own in possible in order to attempt to learn how to upgrade or

raise their this kind of themselve owning capability to be raised to super talent capability level, e.g. some super talent pinano music tool player, when he/she feels interest to play pinano music tool, then he/she will spend extra time to learn how to play this kind of pinano music
tool in order to create many good pinano music to let audiences to listen. They do not feel formal education training method can
raise their playing pinano music tool skill. They choose to learn from themselves at home in their extra time. So, non formal education learning method has more successful chance to train one common pinano music player to be one super talent pinano music player to compare formal education learning method consequently.

Hence, young people need know how to create and innovate their capacities by themselves. This positive attitude is important in enhancing young peoples' innovative and creative potential in ways that are relevant to employability. It seems that non-formal learning method can support innovation and creativity in young people to their undiscovered capabilities to be upgraded or raised. Any countries government need to spend time to invest non-formal
education method to raise young people to discover and learn what their talent capabilities are. The non-formal eduational talent young capabilities plan aims and strategies and outputs may include as below:

It's goals is investment in non-formal learning , leadning to increased capacity for innovation and creativity in young people in ways relevant to employability,
enhancing user-freindly and efficient procedures and methods for recognition of non-formal learning in the development of innovation and creativity skills.

Targets set with indicators to provide signs of progress achievement. The implementing strategies can support non-formal education workers, especially youth workers, who work directly with young people, to raise the quality of provision, such as improving the recognition and validation of non-formal learning, providing (AI) artificialintelligent , robust and accessible tools and resources to support the talent young people capabilities discovering work. Developing partnership working relationship between business and the formal education and non-formal sector, closing the gap between requirements of the labour market and
the contribution of no-formal school learning, enhancing entreprensurial skills in young people.

In conclusion, non-formal school or non-formal training learning method or student himself/herself learning method can bring outputs to manufacture or create super talent young peron more easily to compare formal school learning method, e.g. one school teach 100 students, it won't create any one super talent capability of student easily. Otherwise, 100 young people who can spend extra time to learn how to upgrade or raise themselves owning capabilities at home. Any of one or more than one these 100 young people will have more chance to learn to become one super talent person who owns this kind of capability by himself/herself in success when he/she can accept to spend long time to learn by himself/herself. The reaons is that teachers can not persuade they discover to learn themselves capabilities more easier from themselves. So, one non-formal learning method can achieve these outputs, such as improved procedures and better use of non-formal learning method to measure and accredit non-formal learning, better use of methods to measure and access formal learning , improved provision of training and support for non-formal education workers, effective partnership between labour market and education (formal and non-formal) sectors, promotion of non-formal learning through financial support , technical advice, networks and databases, experiments to develop specific areas of practice. However, instead of young people need to spend time to discover what themselves interests or

capabilities are and learn them, the another most importance to achieve non-formal education method successful factor is that the expert group will assist itself country

government to work with formal and non-formal partners to ensure that ideas from social scientific research, literature, practice wisdom, policy and discovering any kind of capability consultation processes, inform understandings of any individual young person problems, situations and issues, as well as ideas about work that can enable desired outcomes and ways of monitoring and evaluating any individual young person himself/herself " capability discovery work" in order to create talent young person mission in success.

CHAPTER FOUR

Employee Psychological Research Method

Employee satisfaction measurement

● How to measure employee satisfaction ?

It has close relationship between employee satisfaction and work motivation. The right staff can work in the right position which can affect the effective productivity of the company. Also, if employees feel satisfactory , then the company can have more chance to raise (increase) productivity, responsiveness, quality amd good customer service performance. However, if any company want employees to work efficiently, then which needs to know that one of the biggest internal strength of the organization is the relationship and communication between employees and the managers. Besides, the biggest improvement is also needed in the field of the financial rewards, because most of the employees are not showing high satisfaction to them.

Whether how to measure what the level of employee satisfaction is accepted to achieve the stable productivities? The main subjects will be leadership and motivaton to answer this question. For example, supermarket organization, whether which factors could be improved in the target work in supermarket organization every day? I shall assume it has perhaps to cause job dissatisfaction if the supermarket has only the power of money as motivator in supermarket organization. Any organization has its culture. As supermarket organization has also itself culture. However, I believe that cultural traits that can affect the employee satisfaction in any supermarket organizations. Although, any supermarket organization has usually different departments to cooperate work together. Hence, if it has good organizational culture to make different departments, e.g. store, food, wine, stationery, clerical, counter etc. departments staff who can have good communication to work in comfortable cultural supermarket environment together, then its staff can have more ability to achieve the best work performance. How to solve this department cultural difference of challenge, I suggest any supermarket needs have good HRM plan to control its department's employee behaviors.

Human resource means the staff who work in a organization and the contribution who make with whose skill, knowledge and competence. The most important successful factor of knowledge based economy in which intelligent organizations are the key aspects of economic growth in the global economy. Why does organization need to satisfy employee needs? Because any staff trend to change working places often, any staff can change their workplaces to gain more respect and to feel more valued in their jobs. So, it can avoid staff turnover (leaving) whose organization very easy if the employer can satisfy whose staff needs. Thus, human resource plan is needed to achieve policies, recruiting and selecting work force, training and development, workplace planning, ensuring fair treatment of employees, ensuring equal opportunities, assessing the performance of employees, managing employee welfare, providing a counseling service for employees, managing the payment and rewards systems, supervising health and safety procedures, disciplining individuals, dealing with dismissal or promotion, negotiation, ensuring the legality of organizations etc. concerning about managing employees' positive psychological issues, in order to build positive emotion to them.

● How can leaders satisfy employee needs?

Any organization needs have good leaders because leaders act to provide satisfaction or more likely to offer means of satisfaction to whose team members. Leaders don't necessarily motivate. A successful leader understands the needs of the others and persuades them to act in a certain way. A good leaders can make whose workers see that following the views of the leader's workers will get the most satisfaction out of their work. However, a person can be motivated without leadership. But leadership, however, can't succeed without the motivation of the follower's side. If a staff has the feeling that who can perform a higher level job, himself/herself who have the motivation to attend courses or train in another way to be able to perform at the required higher levels.

Douglas Mc Gregor's famous classification of theory x versus theory y is applicable for leadership approaches. In general, any staff has two kinds of psychological characteristics of either theory x person or theory y person. Theory x assumes that in general most staff find working distasteful and usually avoid doing it if it is possible . That is why most staff must be controlled and directed, even threatened to perform the way the organizational goals will be reached. Theory x also assumes that staff want to be controlled and directed rather than take responsibility and that staff lack ambition. Otherwise, theory y on the other hand, is more likely to have roots in the recent knowledge of human behavior. It assumes that physical and mental effort in work is as natural as play or rest. So, leaders need to judge whether whole managing staffs (team members) who belong to theory x or theory y kind of staff. Then, who will have more accurate method to lead whose team members easily.

What level of satisfaction to the organization's staff can achieve the best performance. I feel that when the organization can reach the willingness level to be told the extent to which any one of staff has motivation and commitment or self-confidence to accomplish a certain task. So, the willingless level is the most satisfactory maturity level to achieve the best performance psychological factor to any organization. Because of the maturity satisfactory level of employees is high, the employees are both willing and able to do the tasks given more efficient. Otherwise, if the maturity satisfactory level is moderate, leaders can concentrate on the relationship and participate in the decision making and willing processes as workers are able but may be unwilling to complete their tasks. Only a little bit of enouraging is needed. Otherwise, if the maturety satisfactory level is low, workers are willing but may be unable to complete the tasks, so leaders must push to sell the tasks and let the workers do the rest or leaders must tell workers what to do.

In this supermarket organization case, if supermarket's gocery department and logistic department and clerical or cashier departments and fishing/meet etc. department whose employees' maturity satisfactory level is low, then it is possible that who are unable and unwilling to complete whose individual department daily tasks efficiently and these different department managers need to concentrate on both relationship and task aspects to raise whose maturity satisfactory level to be moderate level, even the high level in order to achieve the best performance.

Leaders also need to concern staff job satisfaction issue. Job satisfaction is the reflection of a good treatment. It also can be considered as an indicator of emotioned well being or psychological health, even job satisfaction can lead to behavior by an employee that affects organizational functioning. Furthermore, job satisfaction can be a reflection of organizational functioning. Why can job satisfaction influence any organizational performance? The reason is some people like to work and who find working is an important part of their lives. Some people on the other hand find work unpleasant and work only because who have to do support their lives. However, job satisfaction tells how much people like their job. Job satisfaction is the most studied field of organizational behavior. It is important to know the level of satisfaction at work for many reasons and the results of the job satisfaction studies. In the workers' point of view, it is obvious that feel repected and satisfied at work, it could be a reflection of a good treatment. In the organization's point of view good job satisfaction can lead to better performance of the workers which affects how the result of the organization to achieve its productivities for long term. So, any employer or leader can not neglect whose staff what job satisfaction level to whose staff in any time. In general, if whose staff can not feel job satisaction, who will choose to leave whose current employer more easily.

Raising employee efficiency

● How does one company raise employee efficiency

What makes one company more successful than another? It is possible to conern better products, services, strategies, technologies or perhaps a better cost structure. However, the final source is the best staff performance of good productive factor, because it can cause these result, also employees who are engaged significantly outperform work group and who are tangible asset to raise the company's competitive advantage where employees are the differentiator, engaged employees are the ultimate goal. What factors can affect job satisfaction. I find that agency theory might be helpful to explain how organizations need to think of their human resource responsible in producing the output needed by organizations to meet shareholders value. Agency theory is concerned with issues related to the ownership of the firm when that ownership is separated from the day-to-day running of the organization. It assumes that in all but owner managed organizations, the owner or owners (known is agency theory as the "principle" of an organization must best authority to an agent -corporate management to act on their behalf) Shenkel, R. Gardner, C. (2004, pp. 57-59).

The principle recognises the risk, here and act on the assumption that any agent will look to serve its own as well as the principle interests as it fulfills it contract with that principal. However, this is not the situation in real life situation. As all agents are perceived to be opportunistic. Agency theory is therefore used to analysis this conflict in interest between the principal (shareholders of organizations) and their agents (leaders of these organizations). The agents in keeping with the interest of the shareholders and organizational goals turn to use financial motivational aspects like bonuses, higher payrolls, pensions, sick allowances, risk payments to reward and retained their staff and enhance their performance. However, given this perception, the principal in an organization will feel unable to predict an agent's behavior in any given situation and so brings into play various measures to do with incentives in other to tie employee's needs to those of their organization. However, the fundamental problem, dealt with is that drives or induces people to exploit their potential resources in the way they do in organization. The issue of motivation and performance are who positively related. By focusing on the financial aspect of motivation problem likes bonus system, allowances perks, salaries etc. I believe financial motivation and trying to Mallow's Basic needs non financial aspect why comes in when financial motivation has failed. So, employers need to evaluate the methods of performance motivation in whose organization in organizing some motivational factors like satisfies and dissatisfies will be used to evaluate how employees motivation is enhanced other, than financial aspects of motivation. I believe that with the changing nature of the work force, recent trends in development, information and technology, the issue of financial motivation becomes consent on one of the most important assets in an organization. The potential role of money is as conditioned reinforce and an incentive which is capable of satisfying needs and an anxiety reducer and serves to erase feelings of dissatisfaction.

In general, any organization can use performance or efficiency to measure its productivities. Such as, performance means the act of performing; of doing something successfully; using knowledge as distinguished from merely possessing it; a performance comprises an event in which generally one group of staff (the performer or performers) behave in a particular way for another group its staff.

Efficiency means the ratio of the output to the input of any system. Economic efficiency is a general term for the value assigned to a situation by some measure designed to capture the amount of waste or friction or other undesiable and undesirable economic feature present. It can also be looked as a short run criterion of effectiveness that refers to the ability of the organization to produce outputs with minimum use of inputs.

Why does employer need to know how to motivate whose staff? What is meaning of motivation? Motivation means as the psychological process that give behavior purpose and direction to behave in a purposive manner to achieve specific unmet needs, an unsatisfied need, and they will to achieve respectively. So, salary, job satisfaction, job goal , reward will be task -related motivation since goals direct staffs' thoughts and action. So, motivation to staff needs have these factors expected. For example, phychological needs are the bottom of the staff, such as foods, air, water and shelter. Any staff needs a salary that enable then to afford adequate living conditions. Then, staffs need safety, psychological needs. They need to work for a secure working environment free from any threats or harms and organizations can provide these need by providing employees, with safety working equipment e.g. hardhars, health insurance plans, fire protection etc. Next, staffs need social needs and the needed to be loved and accepted by other people. Esteem includes the need for self-respect and approval of others. Finally, self actualisation is the top psychological need, it is capable of being to develop the staff himself/herself full potential. The rationale holds to the point that self actualised employees repect valuable assets to the organization human resource.

Why do employers need to concern flexible working arrangement? Employers need to concern flexible working arrangement if who hope employees can raise productivities and efficiencies to achieve the best work performance. Flexible working describes any types of working arrangement that gives some degree of flexibility on how long, where and when employees work. Because employees need time to learn a familiar phase with workplaces, flexible working arrangements have been an option in many employment sectors for a long time, helping employment meets the changing needs of their customers and staff. The reasons include customers expect to have products and services available outside of the traditional 9 to 5 working hours; employees want to achieve a better balance of between work and home life and organizations want to meet their customers and employees needs in a way that enables them to be as productive as possible.

Organizations need to produce any products and services of the right quality and at the right price, under constant pressure. To meet customers' demands, sometimes new ways of working have to be found to make the best use of staff and resources. Flexible patterns of work can help to solve those pressures by maximising the available labor and improving customer service.

At employers, organizations also have a duty of care to protect whose staff from risks to their health and safety, e.g. stress caused by working long hours or feeling pressure to need to balance work and home life. However, flexible working can help to improve the health and wellbeing of employees and by extension, reduce absenteeism, increase productivity, and enhance employee engagement and loyalty. Flexible working time includes per time works often used in hotels, restaurants, warehouses etc. flexitime. Mostly used in office based environments for staff below managerial level in public and private sector service organizations; annualised hours often used in manufacturing and agriculture where there can be big variations in demand throughout the year.

Thus, I feel the flexible working and work life balance benefits can include a more efficient and productive organization, a more motivated workforce, better retention of valuable employees, a wider pool of applicants can be attracted for vacancies, reduced levels of absence and increased customer loyalty and working hours that the best suit the organization, its employees and its customers applications of knowledge about how people as indicators and groups, act within the total organization, analyzing the external environment's effect on the organization and its human resources, missions, objectives and strategies. So, it concerns how to predict staff psychological feeling to learn how to motivate who to work efficiently.

Why does manager need to concern employee's individual diversity need? Also, manager needs to know each person is substantically different from all others in terms of their personalities, needs, demographic factors and past experiences and/or because who are placed in different physical settings, time periods or social surroundings. This diversity needs to be recognized and viewed as a valuabe asset to organizations. Selective perceptions may lead be misinterprectation of single event work or create a barrier in the search for new experience. Managers need to recognize the perceptual differences aiming the the employees and manage them accordingly. These whole person effects between the work life and life outside work and mangagement's focus should be in developing not only a better employee but also better person in terms of growth and fulment. If the whole person can be developed, then benefits will beyong the firm into the larger society in which each employee lives. Because individual's behavior are guided by their needs and the consequences that results from their acts. In case of needs, people are motivated not by what others think who ought to have but by what who themselves went. However, motivation of employee is essential to the operation of organizations and the biggest challenge faced by managers. Organizations ought give more opportunities to let employees who can contribute their talents and ideas because many employees actively seek opportunities at work to become relevant decisions the stay or leave the organization, also managers ought concern any employee's individual skills and abilities and to be provided with opportunities to develop themselves.

Organizational behavior theory

- What is system approach?

What is system approach? All parts of an organization interact in a complex relationship. Systems approach takes an across, the board view of people in organizations and analyses issues in terms of total situations and as many factor as possible that may effect people's behavior. Three theoretical frameworks, the cognitive behavioristic and social learning frameworks, the basis of any organizational behavior model. The cognitive approach is based on the staff and organization expectancy, demand and incentive concepts. Because staff behavior on the basis of the connection between stimulus and response in any organization. The social learning approach incorporates the concepts and principle of both the cognitive and behavioristic frameworks. In this approach, staff behavior is explained as a continuous interaction between cognitive is explained as a continuous environmental determinants. In the organizational behavioral model, there are some dependent variables like productivity, absenteeism turnover, job satisfaction, deviane absenteeism, turnover, organizational citizenship behavior etc. The reason of which staff try to understand. The cause of these outcomes like with some variables of individual, groups and individual level, these variables are called independent variables.

It seems different organizational workplace environments will influence staff's different variable causes to decide how to do whole daily behaviors, how to fit to work in the organization. So, any manager needs to know what every staff is individual characteristics to judge how to manager himself/ herself. For example, if the staff is thoery x person, who will dislikes work and will avoid it if possible, who lacks responsibility, has little ambition and seeks security above all who must be controlled, threatened with punishment to get who to work. So, the manager's attitude is needed to control whom. Otherwise, if the staff is theory y person, who will feel work is as natural as play as rest. People are not inherently lazy,who have become the way is as a result committed, the staff has potential, under proper condition who learn to accept and seek responsibility, who has imagination creativity that can be applied to work, so manageer who is to develop the potential to the staff and help who release that potential toward common objectives.

Any organization depends on the external environment for two kinds of into outputs, which it transforms into outputs and then releases in the hope that external environment will accept them. First, human input, employees and natural resources. Second, non human inputs, e.g. equipment, information, raw materials. However, organization needs to adjust to environmental demands, e.g. customer complaints, market research, financial reports, in order to keep to improve performance easily.

How to raise organizational efficiency? As systems theory indicates organizational effectiveness and time is considered as one element of a larger system of number of elements. The organization takes resources (inputs) from the external environment, processes these resources and returns them in changed form (output). According to system theory, effectiveness criteria must reflect the entire input process, output cycle, not simply output and must also reflect the interrelationships between the organization and its outside environment. In relation to environmental circumstances organization passes through different phases of lifecycle like forming, developing , maturing and declining and the appropriate criteria of effectiveness must reflect the stage of the organization's life cycle.

The criteria of effectiveness are also time based short run (results of actions concluded in a year or less), intermediate run (when effectiveness of individual, group or organization is considered for a longer period, perhaps five years and long run for this the time frame is indefinite future. The four short run effectiveness criteria are quality, productivity, efficiency and satisfaction. Three intermediate criteria are quality, adaptiveness, efficiency amd satisfaction. The two long run criteria are quality and survival. So, any organization needs have effectiveness criteria because effectiveness criteria can reflect the stage is of the organization's life-cycle (which includes stages of growth, maturation and decline) and short, intermediate and long term perspectives. Quality means the total quality control rank among the most used programs to meet customers' changing demand. Hence, employee's indiviaual satisfaction will influence productivity. Because productivity reflects the relationship between the organization's inputs and outputs and measures of productivity include profit, sales, market share. For example, patients released, clients served concerns the relationship between employees' satisfaction and clients' overall satisfaction. When the employee feel more satisfactory, then who will work more efficient or who will serve the clients more pleasant. Then, the customers will have more chance to feel more satisfactory from the staff's individual service.

Efficiency is the ratio of outputs to inputs. It focuses on the entire input process output cycle, emphazing inout and progess. Measures of efficiency include rate of return on capital, or assets, unit cost, waste, downtime, occupancy rates and cost per patient/student etc. customers. Satisfaction meets employee needs. It recognizes the organization is as social system that benefit its participants. Measures of satisfaction include turnover, absenteeism and employee attitudes. Adoptiveness means the degree to which the organization can and does respond to internal and external changes. It relates to management's ability to sense environmental changes and changes within the organizaton. There are no specific measure of adaptiveness, but certain progress, e.g. employee training and career counseling increase its capacity to deal with it. Finally, development means the ability of the organization to increase its capacity to deal with environmental demand. So, if the organization hope to be survival in the long term, then it needs to achieve training programs and organizational development to be represent the organization's investment in survival.

Employee satisfaction methods

- How can satisfy to employees' needs ?

How can satisfy to employees? Because a high rate of employee is directly related to a lower turnover rate. Thus, keeping employees' satisfied with their careers should be a major priority for every employers. Reasons why employees can become discourages with jobs and design, including high stress, lack of communication within the organization, lack of recognition, or limited opportunity for growth. So, management need actively seek to improve these factors to avoid if who hope to lower turnover rate. However, some employee will often be feel bored with the work because there is no intrinsic motivation to succeed. Finding the daily same job duties can reduce the individual's motivation to succeed to raise desire to show up to work and to do the job well. In this case, the employee may continue to come to work, but whose efforts will be minimal.

Stress is another factor to cause low performance. Branham (2005) indicates that " it seems clear that one quarter to one half of all workers are feeling some level of dysfunction, sue to stress, which is undoubtedly have a negative improve on their productivity and the probability that they will stay with their employers."

However, stress can be caused by these factors, e.g. in the situation, when a company can't or won't supply the tools necessary to produce or work efficiently on the job. This produced higher stress levels because these workers are expected to perform at certain rates, yet who are unable to do so. This results in lower productivity and higher turnover because quotes can't be met by the employees. On staff knowing that management is able to provide the tools essential for the position is important to employee trusting the intentions of their employer.

Dissatisfaction with the job many come from sources other than stress or poor fit between employee and the job. Employers that are deemed unethical by workers because who appear to care about company revenues, rather than the employees that are working for them. In the result, the employer may lead to job dissatisfaction, and raise the company's turnover rate.

Lack of communication in the workforce is another major contributor to dissatisfaction. Bad communication leaves employees feeling disconnected from the organizations. This is detrimental to wellbeing of the company because when an employee feels neglected, who will trend to perform at a lower level because who feels unsure of whose position within the company and wonders what whose purpose is within the workplace. Also, employees may be unaware of how whose performance measures up to that of their co-workers and have no sense of who can improve. So, without communication, it becomes difficult for employees to make any progress in their efficiency. The employee may feel uncomfortable in the workplace, of who feel rarely be praises for the quality of whose performance. Finally, those factors cause the failure to provide employees with opportunities to grow within the company results in employee frustration to cause whose poor performance and low productivity.

Whether can bonuses increase raise employee satisfaction and team performance? In some occupations, I feel bonuses can raise staff performance, such as bonuses lead to happier and it can be used in the form of donations to charity organization or bonuses in the form of expenditures to pharmaceutical sales teams and sport teams organizations. However, employees are becoming more and more unhappy, more and more of time at work, hardly a formula for a healthy and productive workplace. In this increasingly negative environment, how can employers incentivize their employees to increase their happiness, job satisfaction, and job performance? Certainly, designing effective incentive schemes is a central challenge for a wide range of organizations form multi-national corporations to academic departments. Identifying the most effective strategies, a variety of incentive schemes and are suggested such as bonuses from fixed salaries to pay-performance from commission to end-of-year bonuses. It is based to assume that the best way to motivate employees is to reward them with money that who then spend on themselves. In general, existing methods of increasing workplace performance, including individual-based and team based bonuses schemes, which trend to reveal both benefits and unexpected cost. Whether the benefits of improving social life in the work phase can increase employee citizenship behaviors to satisfy the organization actual needs from these bonuses compensation schemes.

What is the effect of money on employee's job satisfaction and performance? On one hand, monetary bonuses have been found to have positive effects, increased productivity effort, performance and job satisfaction. Individual bonuses increase job satisfaction in part. On the other hand, individual incentives, such as large bonuses are often surprising ineffective increasingly employee morale and productivity. In an effort to prevent such negative competitive dynamic that can result from individual based-bonuses, organizations often change to incentivize employees for their collective performance, encouraging cooperation and teamwork rather than competition. Otherwise, in some cases, team based compensation schemes have been shown to raise this sense of cooperation between team members, inducing them to exert additional effort toward helping another worker to work together linked to employee morale and performance.

Whether bonuses can have a causal impact on employee. In fact, individual incentives, such as large bonuses are often surprisingly ineffective in increasingly employee morale and productivity. Also, rewarding individual employees can produce negative outcomes, as employees become reluctant to share information with others even at the expense of reduced output. In an effort to prevent such negative competitive dynamics that can result from individual based bonuses. Importantly, such increased cooperation due to interdependent rewards has been shown to improve team performance, suggesting that team based bonuses may be an effective means of improving employee social life. As with individual based bonuses, however team based bonuses offer important advantages, but also potential drawbacks. I suggest that prosocial bonuses can have a causal impact on employee satisfaction and performance, such that providing employees with money to spend on themselves.

How effective organizational communication can affect employee attitude, happiness and job satisfaction. Communication has been studied with regard to performance and job satisfaction, but the relationship with employee attitude and happiness has not been done in a higher education setting. The value of communication in an employee's choice to be happy is explained as it affects the individual, team and overall organizational culture. Attitude and happiness have been recognized by communication examination of organizational culture and emotion in the workplace. For example, for frontline employees are needed have cheerful and positive in the face or any situation. So, it requires the owners, managers and supervisors communicate to whose team efficiently.

Communication with telecommuting or remote workers is a consideration that organizations must take seriously more than 24 million people were working remotely in 2008 year (World at work, 2009) and that number is steadily rising. Teleworkers report feelings of isolation, uncertainty, a lack of trust and lower organizational commitment with lower job satisfaction. Managers may not communicate the save way with remote workers as who do with employees who are in the workplace each day. Improve communication is important to hold employee engagement initiatives together, particularly in government public sector organizations must communicate throughout the entire cycle of planning, conducting and acting on engagement. So, I suggest some effective communication method to raise productivity and improve performance. Such as ensuring that employees understand their work expectation between their jobs and the organization's mission, meeting regularly with staff members, providing feedback as performance , as well as opportunities to grow and developing , even fail as a way to learn and holding employees accountable for performance, including with poor performance.

How to make a difference at work be more meaningful and purposeful workplaces. The workplace provides a wealth of opportunities and possibilities through which anyone can make a difference every day. Whether it's one person, one team or one organization, everyone has the capacity to create positive and meaningful change in their workplace in both small and large ways. How to foster the work motivation of individuals and team? Nowadays, some evidence supports claims that motivational programs can increase the quality and quantity of performance from 20 to 40 percent. Moreover, motivation can solve three types of performance challenges: first, staff are refusing to change often, second, allowing themselves to be distracted and not persist at a key task and/or third, treating a task as familiar, making mistakes but not investing mental effort and taking responsibility because of overconfidence.

Imagine that more than 50% of staff in your organization decided that from this point, who would work one extra day a work without an extra day of rest. What impact would their decision have on your organization's bottom line? What is the value of a 50% increase in performance by 100% of the workforce? Assuming that you may know some of the 50% , who do the minimum and a few of the 80% who could work much harder, do you think that there is anything that would convince people to work harder than who are now? Is it possible that half of your staff who admit that who could work much harder might actually decide to increase whose performance by 20% or more if they were adequately motivated? The best evidence suggests that highly significant performance increases are possible when motivational strategies are implemented (Clark & Estes, 2002).

● How to achieve work motivation strategy ?

Work motivation is the process that initiates and maintains goal-directed performance. Without motivation , even the most capable person will refuse to work hard. Thus, motivational performance gaps exist whenever staff avoid starting something new, resist doing something familiar, stop doing something important or attention to a less valued task, or refuse to work smart on a new challenges, instead use old familiar, but inadequate solutions to solve a new problem (Clark, 1998).

How can we make sense of such variety and get benefits as performance technologies? Is any given situation where we want to increase work motivation, we must determine what will convince staff to start doing something new or different increase their persistence at an important task and investment mental effort. The staff must believe that the motivator driving their enhanced performance will directly or indirectly contribute significantly to what who need to feel successful and effective. The motivator's work has to cost less than the value of the increased performance and it must meet both ethical and legal requirement. When it might appear that solutions have to be tailored to the different demands of individuals in a team. In the absence of a clear vision leading to work defined business and performance goals, people substitute their own goals and whose goals may not support the organization. So, it is important to ask about evidence for the benefit of all work rules and what might be cost of the rules more eliminated. What is gained by rules that staff can't take or eat in certain areas? Why can't they decorate their work space in ways that suit them? How much of staff's behavior must you control to achieve business goals? One way to motivate and staff and simplify organizational work processes is to eliminate all unnecessary rules, policies and procedures.

To learn how to motivate staff, we need to learn how to predict staff's individual psychological behavior. Organizational behavior is a scientific discipline in which large number of research studies and conceptual developments are constantly adding to its knowledge base. It is also an applied science, in that information about effective practices in one organization is being extended to many others. Organizational behavior is the systematic study of human behavior, attitudes and performance within an organizational setting, drawing on theory methods and principles from such disciplines as psychology, sociology and cultural anthropology to learn about individual perceptions, values, learning, capacities and actions when workings in groups .

Nowadays, why employees hope employers can give them to enjoy well life balance. The reasons may include care commitments to children or elderly relatives, education commitment that limit availability at times of the week/month/year, duties and/or interests outsid of work, needing to be available for people making a greater sense of well being and reduced stress levels. How to arrange flexible working in organization? For example, an employer may be thinking about introducing annualised hours in order to increase productiom levels to meet infrequent rises in demand because who can work well where, there are peaks in works, the workforce is required to be available with little notice. The employer could decide to meet these increases in demand by introducing overtime because it provides flexibility to meet fluctuations and it could be a smaller change to the organization than annualised hour. However, there are many different forms of flexible working. Flexible working can cover the way working hours are organised during the day, week or year. It can also describe the place of work, such as homeworking or the kind of contract, such as a temporary contract. Anyway, flexitime can operate in different ways depending on business need. On the one hand, there may be a system to allow employee to build up additional hours, which can be used to leave early, come in late, or take longer periods off with early, come in late, ot take longer periods off, with approval from line management. An example of this might be an assembly line or call centre where staffing must be scheduled to meet customer demand. For example, an employer needs to extend the hours that whose business is open to 8 AM to 8 PM, but can't afford the extra overtime. how to manage flexitime approach could help provide the additional hours, reduce staff numbers at quiet times and minimise the need for overtime. Employer may benefit from the opportunity to travel outside of peak hours and/or accommodate personal responsibilities, such as the school runs part time work is the must common types of flexible working. It's potential benefits include customer demands on be met and machinery can be caused more efficiently if part time workers cover lunch breaks/evening shifts and weekends, the working day can be arranges around caring responsibilities and/or other commitments, employees can continue to work increasing whose own leisure time. But part time work also have potential challenges, such as increase in training, increase in administrative and recruitment costs, e.g. recruiting two part timers could longer than one full times and providing a continuous level of service may be difficult.

Overtime is normally hours that are worked over the usual full time hours. It can be compulsory or voluntary . A recognized system of paid overtime is more common with hourly paid staff than salaried staff. Potential benefits include that employer can provide flexibility to meet fluctuations in demand, short term labor shortage without having to recruit extra staff overtime. Even with premium payments, is often less costly than recruiting and training extra staff or buying extra equipment. However, overtime work has also potential challenges, include when working excessive overtime can affect an employee is performance health and home life. It can result in higher absence levels and unsafe working practices.

Job sharing is a form of part time working where two or more people share the responsibility for a full time job. They share the pay and benefits in proportion to the hours each works. They share the pay and benefits in proportion to the hours each works. Job shares may work split days, split weeks or alternate weeks. it's potential benefits include that if one job sharer is absent, due to illness or holiday, the other can carry on with at least half the work, who can help meet people demand , e.g. both shares being present when workloads are heavy, a wider range of available, who can help people with caring responsibilities and/or other commitments to continue working. It is potential challenges also include extra induction, training and administration cost, replacement may be difficult if one job sharer leaves, added responsibility on supervisors/managers, who must allocate well fairly and ensure that the job shares communicate effectiveness. If the shared role involves managing on supervising staff can find it is difficult working for two managers.

Shift work is a pattern of work in which one employee replace another doing the same job within a 24 hour periods. Shift workers normally work in crews, which are groups of workers who make up a separate shift team. it's potential benefits include it can reduce costs by using equipment more intensively and taking advantage of cheaper off peak. It's potential challenges include it can increase wage and labor costs, it can disrupt employees' social and domestic lives, it can upset employees' body and affect an employee's performance and health.

Employers ought concern employee engagement issue. Different professions have their own specific, which need to be addressed during the engagement building process. For example, for hospital workers, safety issue is of a high importance as who deal with different kinds of sicknesses, whereas for teachers or conselors, ths issue of stress and emotional exhaustion many be of more importance.

To learn how to satisfy employees, content with their work experience, was a good formula for success, as a satisified employees, who wanted to stay with a company, contributed to the workforce stability and productivity. However, satisfied employees may just meet the work demands, but this won't lead to higher performance. In order to compete effectively, employers need to go beyond satisfaction. Therefore, modern organizations expect their employees to be full of enthusiasm to work.

Other researchers state that employee engagements is the best fool in the company's efforts to gain on competitive advantages and stay competition. Though, the notion of engagement is relatively new, and it is already a hot managerial topic and it is rare to find an HR or managerial related acticle that doesn't mention employee engagement. These researchers agree that engagement creates the prospect for employees to attach closely with their managers, co-workers and organization in general and engaging environment is the environment when employees have positive attitude toward their job and are willing to do high quality job.

It seems that how to develop good engagement workplace environment can influence employees' satisfaction, then it can influence whose performance or productivity. So, they have close relationship. however, it is even harder to build engagement within the specific group of employees in the situation, when the knowledge about the specifics of their work-life is missing. Different occupations need have different engagement workplace environments and engagement methods to let employees to feel satisfaction. For example, engagement of administrative workers in the educational organizations is rarely studied and poorly understanding, even though these employees have a significant influence in the institution and the quality of their performance contributes to the quality of relationships with faculty students and the public. So, understanding the administrative personnel work life perception is important to educational organizations. How schools can implement engagement to achieve target to improve administration employees (administrative workers) whose performance, students, faculty public satisfaction and other organizational outcomes. Because whose performance is not save to factory workers to cause how many product quantities manufacturing per hour to calculate, whose need to use service quality to measure performance.

I feel it is better in the situation when organizattions have a better understanding of the administrative personnel work-life perceptions, it is easier for them to create appropriate engagement building tools. Such as, administration employees working at small sized education organizations are more engaged, and this might be due to the reason that they have better relationships with colleagues and experience a greater sense of belonging than their colleages from larger education organizatins. Futhermore, Johnsrud and Rosser (1999) also suggest that the smaller the institution, the more positive administrative workers moral and consequentially the higher chances for their engagement. Therefore, result of this study can be applied only to the educational institutions of the similar size. Furthermore, results of this study can't be used for similar organization in order contributions.

What factors can influence the engagement of administration staff. I feel that significant variables factors include: working conditions, job fit, role fit, time spent interacting with students and length of employment on campus. As some researchers working conditions were found to be a significant and positive factor influencing engagement, this means that better working conditions increase the chance that the employee will shoe in higher level of engagement person job fit was defined by Edwards (1991, as referenced in Kristof, 1996, p.8) as " the fit between the abilities of a person and the demands of a job , i.e. demands-abilities or the desires of a person and the attributes of a job needs supplies". Job fit also focuses more on the formal aspects of the work, when role-fit includes both established and new tasks, which core out in teams, as team members‘ roles include formal tasks as well as informal socially defined tasks. The only factor , which was found to have a negative influence on the engagement of administrative workers was employment history, meaning that the higher level of employees were working within an educational organizaton, the lower level of engagement who showing.

I shall recommend to measure the engagement level of employees and to find out the specific engagement that need to be improved, the quantitative research with questionnaires as the main source collecting data was needed to choose to any educational organizations. Because questionnaires can produce numberical data, which is a quantitative approach. The educational administrative workers can be compared with each other within the category of engagement and can point out the factors driving engagement, which need to be improved. These numbers are the basis for further analysis and recommendations. The factors, which can be chosen for the investigation, include meaningful job autonomy at work, performance feedback, institution development opportunities, organizational support, procedural justice, social support from colleagues, supervisory support, social climate etc. The reasons to choose these factors to investigate because the meaningful job can increase psychological meaningfulness for the employee and therefore increases engagement.The above factor meaningful job has been included in the list. Besides, job characteristics can increase meaningfulness for the employee and are positively rarely to job engagement. However, educational administrative workers' moral has an influence on their perception an attitude to the job. The same study pointed out that the moral of administrative workers in educational organization is influenced by number of factors, such as working atmosphere, relations with colleagues and supervisors. For example, social support from colleagues and supervisory support is concerned to moral issue. Social climate factor is concerned to reward and recognition issue.

Why employers need to concern employee moral issue. For example, any clinic organization has complex interpersonal relationships within the clinical domain and thc critical issues are faced by nurses on a daily basis, indicate that morale, job satisfaction and motivation are essential components in improving workplace efficiency, output and communiction amongst staff. Drawing on educational , organizational and psychological research, that the ability to inspire morale, staff morale which is a fundamental indicator of sound leadership and managerial characteristics. These includes role preparation for managers, understanding internal and external motivation, how internal motivation to nursing staff and the importantce of attitude when investing in relationships. Because this factors can influence nurse performance. As the field of nursing, amongst money others, the concepts of developing emotional self-awareness in staffs, self-control, adaptability in initiating in management, and organization teamwork in social networks have been poorly applied. Despite this, it has been suggested that nurse and physican collaboration is one of three strongest predictors of psychological empowerment of nurses (Larrabee et. 2003).

Relationships on the ward can influence to nurse satisfaction and personal professionals are closely linked to self-esteem or person's own morale. So, morale of nurse occupation can influence performance to serve patients. In health care industries, how to create healthy working clinical environments and encourage nursing staff for leadership and management roles, the issues of morale and motivation need to become primary concerns in the ward setting. Because any nurse service will fill with dread, fear and anxiety to whose patients if who neglects to concern care morale. So, nurses need to concern motivating behavior and discourages pessimistic feelings and performance. The reality is that some people naturally posses a high level of this internal motivation, these who focus on the internal feelings of satisfaction who will attain despite any difficulties who face along the way. Exceutives are coached, athletes are coached, why not health care professionals? The nature of helping others through clinical care provision may preclude staff from asking for help themselves.

Has it relationship between boosting morale and improving performance in the nursing occupation? For example, healthy working environment and system may be assisted through the regularity of coaching key staff, e.g. nurses in hospitals need to create any clinic ward organizations. Clinical will environments with good retention, work satisfaction and high quality measures. Nurses can also learn how to self-coach be more self aware and develop themselves. In the nursing occupation, linking nurses‘ daily work to long term ambitions will impose their motivation, boost their self-confidence and assist them to function at a higher performance level. Coaching will also help staff recognise their own management styles, and identify their leadership strengths and areas for improvement. Because nursing work is frequently rewarded by patients' gratitude. Nurses within clinical settings often comment on the patients‘ capacity to say thank you and their appreciation of how nurses contribute to their well being. So, the success of their health care service. In fact, performance appraisal is ideally about recognising the direction an individual nurse wishes to pursue concern how health care moral behavior to nurses to achieve to satisfy patient's individual need to reduce complaint occurrences to build healthy clinic environment to let nurses to work enjoyable.

Why absenteeism will influence performance? Unscheduled absenteeism is a popular problem for U.S. employers, conservatively costing $3,600 per hourly employee per year and $2,650 per salaries employee per year, the majority of employers have limited ability to accurately and regularly track how much absenteeism is reducing their bottom line earning, effective absence management systems can track absenteeism, manage absence policies and work schedules, and control overtime, allowing management to reduce lost earnings, also reducing absenteeism will also help employers better meet production and service demands without requiring an increase in headcount. Commonly, the unschedules absenteeism rate in the U.S. hourly workforce is approximately 9% almost one in ten workers is absent when who woud be at work. There are considerble direct and indirect costs are increasing. Not only should managers be motivated to reduce absenteeism because of the excss costs, but without absence tracking tools, employers can't adequately estimate their accurated liabilities. However, absenteeism causing is probable due to poor health to the individual employee. So, who will perform poorly to influence whose productivity to be worse. Why is there such little focus on absenteeism, compared to other costs, health care or low productivity or poor service performance costs for example? So absenteeism can raise much different workforce related costs. The excess costs arise cause disruption to the business, make it difficult to deloy the workforce, and have a profound effect productivity, profit margins and poor employee morale.

However, improving employee health can at most, only reduce absenteeism by one-third, as two-thirds of absenteeism is caused with non-sickness (personal reasons, feeling of entitlement, family issues). In the result, the direct impact is reduced or poor delayed production or customers are not being served. How to solve absenteeism challenges? Generally, the employer was using a five day schedule, but demand was such that employees were asked to come in on the weekend on a regular basis. The employees disliked working, so many consecutive days with no time off, which led to very high absence rates. The shortages of employees results in demand not being met and customers were dissatisfied. The organization has to replace missing workers with other employees or contractors and pay overtime or higher rates. Overtime levels are 28% higher in facilities with low absenteeism. Excess staffing plan, such as headcount is higher than necessary in order to cover unplanned absences. For example, the employer routinely increased headcount by 13% on weekends to copr with extra absenteeism on a Saturday and Sunday. It is less usual for a salaried employee to be replaced when absent. Instead, the demands of customers (internal or external) are not met and depending on the employee's position in the company, the ability to create revenue may be affected. Excess absenteeism can also lead to increased health care cost, greater safety issues and accidents, high turnover, and poor morale or performance. To achieve significant reductions in the excess costs with absence, the manager must reduce the rate of absenteeism and the subsequent effect that absenteeism hasno the business. The first step is accuratey and efficiently tracking absenteeism rates and pattrens on a regular basis. The majority of organizations don't hae an automated means to track every instance of absence in one system and therefore lack the visibility necessary to address this business problem. Once the root causes of the problem are known. The manager can consider what steps need to be taken. There may include using rules engines and process automation to consistently enforce absence policies, compliance with union, state and rules, improving absence management technology and increasing employee satisfaction with the workplace, reducing overtime costs by selecting employee to cover for absence based on their competence, training and hours worked during the week, accurate reports of absenteeism , patterns over time and root causes.

In order to take full advantage of opportunities for business expansion and growth. Human assets investment strategy is very important to any organizations. For example, airport organization, it needs good employees serve to provide excellent customer services to satisfy the increase flight slots at airports. So good human assets investment strategy can drive focus on safety, innovation and globalization and create programs for motivating employees to enable them to fully demonstrate their abilities. Such as airport training is needed to be given by lecturers, include rank based and elective training to airport service industry. Methods are such as on site courses, supporting the career development to any airport different rank of staffs to promote on environment where individual employees can display their capabilities to the maximum possible extent in their repective roles. In special, giving women career training establishing a mentor system under which senior employees provide ongoing direction and support for junior and new employees and introducing role models through an intranet, supporting for working includes holding seminars for woman who are pregnant or on maternity leave and introducing a system or partical employment. As a result, the number of employee and nearly all of tem return to the workforce. Because airport service industry needs have a large female workforce, including cabin attendants and airport passenger service staff. Besides, airport service industry also needs to hire women for career track administrative and maintenance positions and flight crews and working to increase the percentage of women in management positions.

Better work life balance is also needed to satisfy airport service industry staff. Besides, airport service industry also needs to hire women for career track administrative and maintenance positions and flight crews and working to increase the percentage of women in management positions. Because airport job duty is common needed to be shift duty. Hence, the working time is flexible time to work when new employees decide to attribute to airport service career. However, due to many passengers need, so airport service workers need to work overtime hours. But, commonly, who do not hope to work overtime often. So, airport management needs to create an comfortable and enjoyable working environment in which each new or old employee can rethink whose own working style to contribute will help vitalize society, companies and individuals.

How to leverage technology to improve employee engagement? Nowadays, employee engagement has evolved from a relatively unknown trend to a term in common usage, which leads itself to a variety of forms and levels of understanding. Employee engagement is about the ability of leaders to inspire their people around the way forward at the desired pace, involving a planned communication effort that is integrated with all the other leadership and change activites. Employee engagement is the emotional commitment the employee has to the organization and its goals. However, technology can play an important role in making engagement a practical part of everyday work. As companies move towards a digital workplace, understanding the impact of technology on employee engagement is critical.

What is the digital workplace? The digital workplace is the digital environment in which staff work, and a place to find corporate knowledge. It includes a collection of election tools that enable productive, effective, work from anywhere. In the future, according to the workplace of the future survey by Teknion corporation predicted 88% of companies offer their workforce personal devices, such as smartphones and tablets. Nearly 90% of companies plan to increase their investment in productivity enabling technologies, such as voice activation and video conferencing by 20 15 year. Organizations are seeking the difital workplace as which search for ways to be more efficient, more collaborative and reduce their physical workplace to realizing higher levels of productivity with their workforce. So, it seems digital workplace can assist to raise performance. Two important reasons why new technology tools will be represent great return on investment for internal use with employees.

The first reason is technology helps us comment with and engage remote or disconnected employees, those with little or no computer or internet access during their work time . The second reason is peer-to-peer engagement and using technology can drive the generation of more ideas, which drives innovation and improvement to produce in any workplace. So, creating an actionable roadmap that fully technology in sny organization's staff engagement initiatives can improve bottom line performance. So, technology can assist organization to measure employee engagement, connect disconnected workers, envourage collaboration and social interaction.

I assure engagement lies in sound decision making and action, then driving good decision making and action should be a communicator's core strategy. Many communicators are already doing good work to drive action. Then, good decision making is driven, in part, by the availability f good information. Even employees who are less digitially connected at work can contribue great ideas that improve that work situation and organizational productivity. Examples, of ways technology helps to that such as: one employee posts about a project who is working on, another employee in an office on the other side ot the world sees the post and realizes who is working on a similar project. If the two teams combine their effort, who can solve the problem and the company gets a globl solution. So, corporate internet is a new digital workplace tools. To effectively solve challenge as making the right information available to the right people at the right time. Organizations must begin by clearly identifying the core types of information that must be shared to engage employee and bring about maximum organizational benefit.

What critical organizational information should all employees access? What types of knowledge are suitable for collaboration? What informational exist today and how are these pockets of information affecting business performance? When analyzing your environment for knowledge sharing, take the time to understand knowledge sharing objectives and how to get employees on information that empowers them to be more successful and therefore more engaged. Remember, anyone can serve in this knowledge management role as long as who are contributing relevant and engaging information.

When looking at any new technology to improve organization knowledge transfer and employee engagement for your employees you should conside the following questions: How does the proposed technology create for information sharing? Are they create for information sharing? Are they easy to use for people of all levels of the organization? How does the technology solution you are examing help employees get work accomplished? This is especially important when examining enterprise social technologies. How can the technology provide more information about company vision, people, business processes. How effectively does the technology support key organizational scenarios, such as identifying the best talent for a particular department or initiative? For example, hospital environment can give conversation about the patient benefits of a new in-room online information display at a hospital.

- How can influence organizational positive behaviors ?

Nowadays, there are key forces are affecting daily organizational behaviors and continuing challenges, such as staff structure (work relationship), technology (resources inputs)are needs to transform to with people work and affects the tasks that who perform, environment (internal and external) factors influence the attitudes of staff, affect working conditions and provide competiton for resources and power. So, based on these four forces, managers need to face the different challenges, such as managing chances in a global environment, managing ethical issues at work.

How to raise staff performance to satisfy clients' needs? Customer service and satisfaction is not limited to the private sector, public sector also needs , e.g. education reform, privatizatin, managed case. So, staff need have excellent performance to raise quality of service to satisfy students, patients etc. needs. Why organizations focus on customer satisfaction. Business monitor customer satisfaction in order to determine how to increase customer base, customer loyalty, revenue, profit, market share and survival. Besides, government needs to monitor monitor customer satisfaction to achieve citizen needs. What is customer satisfaction? Customer satisfaction can be experienced in a variety of situations and connected to both products and services. It is a highy personal assessment that is greatly affected by customer expectations, satisfaction also is based on the customer's experience of both contact with the organization , the moment of touth and personal outcomes. Private sector means it is as one who receives significant added value as well as public sector means it is to whose bottom line. However, customer satisfaction differs depending on the situation and the product or service. A client may be satisfied with a product or service on experience, a purchase decision, a salesperson, store, servicce provider or an attitude. So, staff performance can influence or client's decision to choose to buy the product or consume the service indirectly. For example, in hospital organization , patient surveys often ask customers to rate their providers and experiences in response to detailed questions, such as " How well did your physicians keep you informed?" These surveys provide "actions" data that reveal obvious steps for improvement.

Client satisfaction is highly personal assessment that is greatly influenced by individual expectation. In the public sector, the definition of client satisfaction is often linked to both the personal interaction with the service provider and the outcomes experiences by service users. For example, satisfaction with client worker interaction whether in person, by phone, or by mail or by email communication, satisfaction with the support payment , e.g. its accuracy and timeliness ans satisfaction with the effect of child support enforcement on the child. For hospital organization, staff performance need have these service quality factors to raise or improve whose service satisfaction experience to whose patients (clients), e.g. timeliness and convenience, personal attention, reliability and dependability, employee competence and professionalism, empathy, responsiveness, assurance, availability and tangible, such as physical facilities and equipment and the appearance of the personnel.

Satisfaction and engagement are two important distinct mesurements that provide valuable and actionable insights into the workforce. The problem is that how many organizations still view them as one and th same thing. As a result, they may be missing critical opportunities to foster the kind of workforce engagement that drives innovtion, boosts performance and increases competitive success. However, some organizations think which don't have to worry about engagement because turnover is how and employees seem satisfied when employee satisfaction is important to matintaining a positive work environment. Is it enough to help you retain top performers and drive bottom line impact? Probably not, by focusing more employee engagement, organizations are more likely to maintain a strong, motivated workforce that is willing to expand extra effort, drive business goals and deliver a return on HR's talent management investment. How to acheve actionable strategies for maximizing workforce engagement and subsequently, driving higher perfomance across the organization. It addresses critical questions, such as: Do you want satisfied employees or engaged employees? Which has a greater impact on the organization's bottom line? What are some proven techniques for addressing both satisfaction and engagement? Employee satisfaction can typically measued through surveys to gsther opinions about HR related issues like bonus programs, benefits and work/life balance. Som employee satisfaction can refer to how employees feel, that happiness about their job and conditions, such as compensation, benefits, work environment, career development opportunities. On the other hand, engagement refers to employees commitment and connection to work as measured by the amount of discretinary effort, who are willing to expand discretionary effort, who are willing to expand on behalf of their employer. High engaged employees go above and beyond the core responsibilities outlines in their job descriptions, innovating and thinking outside the box to move their organizations forward, much like volunteers are willing to give their fine and energy to support a cause about which they are truly passionate.

Can an organization have a satisfied employee who isn't engaged? Chances is an engaged employee is also a satisfied employee. However, it is certainly possible to have a satisfied employee a with a low engagement level. That's why focusing on satisfaction without addressing engagement is unlikely to foster the kind of expectional workforce performance that drives business results. Why do organizations need to care about their workforce engagement level? The primary goal of a business is to make money, even non profit organizations exist to fund their specific causes. Many studies have linked organizations need to get employees at all levels focused on driving revenue. Also which indicates to link employee engagement to workforce preference, customer satisfaction, productivity absenteeism, turnover. Employee engagement is a concept that is rooted in science and at the most fundamental level reflects the human condition itself.

It makes sense that this human motivation process would apply in the workplace just as in other areas of life. By motivating employees beyond basic satisfaction to achieve higher levels of engagement. HR professionals have more significantly impact business outcomes and drive bottom line results. Top-performing organizations understand that measuring employees' contentment levels and emotionl commitment to the organization on a regular basis can put them at a competitive advantage. Since satisfaction measures on employee happiness with current job and security opportunities to use skills and abilities, the organiztion's financial stability, relationship with immediate supervisor, compensation and benefits. In general, these factors can contribute to job satisfaction, such as job security, opportunities to use skills and abilities, organization's financial stability, relationship with immediate supervisor compensation and benefit, communication between employees and senior management, the work itself, autonomy and independence, management's recognition of employee preformance. However, fact engagement condition can have these difference with job satisfaction, such as relationship with co-workers, opportunities to use skills and abilities relationship with immediate supervisor, contribution of work to organization's business goal, meaningfulness of job, variety of work, overll corporate cultures. In general, staff tend to receive more pleasure and satisfaction from what who do if who are in jobs or roles that match both their interests and skills if staff feel who are making meaningful contributions to whose jobs, thei organizations do society as a whole, they tend to be more engages. Staff want to be recognized and rewarded for their contributions. Rewards and recognition come in many forms, including competitive compensation packages, a healthy work/life balance, or sales trips etc. benefits. So, lack of motivation will affect productivity. In addition, a number of point to low morale: declining productivity, higher incidence of absenteeism and friendness, increasing defective products higher number of accidents or a higher level of waste materials and scrapes. How much money (salary) will you give to your employee to satisfy whose needs? However, staff's needs differ some can be motivated by opportunity for growth and development, job security, good working condition moew than high salary.

In conclusion, as a manager, if you want to develop and encourage good employee performance, and good performance comes from strong employee motivation. But managers can't motivate employee. Motivation is an internal state, like emotions and attitudes, that only the individual can control. Managers can however, create a workplace environment to attempt to motivate staff. Nowadays, workplace is affected by a number of factors, includng a decreasing emphasis on money, an increasing amount of work, an increasing need to work together in teams. Hence, employers concern to consider these above different psychological factors which can influence employee's individual behavior to perform efficiently in any organization.

Reference

Branham, L. (2005). The 7 Hidden Reasons Employees Leave: How To Recognize The Subtle Signs And Act Before Its Too Late. New York, NY: Amacom.

Clark, R.E. (1998). Motivating Performance, Performance Improvement, 37 (8), 39-47.

Clark, R.E. & Estes, F. (2002). Turning Research Into
Results: A Guide To Selecting The Right Performance Solutions. Atlanta, G.A: CEP Press.

Johnsrud, L.K. and Rosser, V.J., 1999. College and
University Midlevel Administrators:
Explaining and improving their morale. The
review of higher education, 22(2), pp. 121-141.

Kristof, A.C. 1996. Person-organization fit: An
Integrative Review of its conceptualizations, measurement and implications. Personnel psychology, 49(1), pp.1-49.

Larrabee J.H. Janney M.A., Ostrow C.L., Withrow M.L., Hobbs G.R. And Burant C. (2003) Predicting registered nurse job satisfaction and intent to leave., Journal of nursing administration, 33 (5), 271-283.

Shenkel, R. & Gardner, C. (2004), " Five ways to retain good staff", Family Management, Now-Dec. , pp.57-59.

World at work (2009). Telework trend lines. Retrieved from http://www.workingfromanywhere.org/News/Trend lines_2009.pdf

www.ingramcontent.com/pod-product-compliance
Ingram Content Group UK Ltd.
Pitfield, Milton Keynes, MK11 3LW, UK
UKHW041641190726
13854UKWH00006B/2634